Big BAD Book of BART SIMPSON™

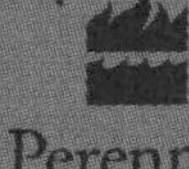

Perennial
An Imprint of HarperCollinsPublishers

In memory of Dan DeCarlo:

Comic book legend, mentor, and friend.

BIG BAD BOOK OF BART SIMPSON

HarperCollins books may be purchased for educational, business, or sales promotional use. For information please write: Special Markets Department, HarperCollins Publishers Inc., 10 East 53rd Street, New York, NY 10022.

FIRST EDITION

ISBN 0-06-055590-4

03 04 05 06 07 08 QWM 10 9 8 7 6 5 4 3 2

Publisher: MATT GROENING
Creative Director: BILL MORRISON
Managing Editor: TERRY DELEGEANE
Director of Operations: ROBERT ZAUGH
Special Projects Art Director: SERBAN CRISTESCU
Art Director: NATHAN KANE
Production Manager: CHRISTOPHER UNGAR
Legal Guardian: SUSAN A. GRODE

Trade Paperback Concepts and Design: SERBAN CRISTESCU

Contributing Artists:
IGOR BARANKO, KAREN BATES, JOHN COSTANZA, DAN DECARLO, MIKE DECARLO, LUIS ESCOBAR, TIM HARKINS, CHIA-HSIEN JASON HO, NATHAN KANE, MIKE KAZALEH, CAROLYN KELLY, LEE LOUGHRIDGE, SCOTT MCRAE, BILL MORRISON, KEVIN M. NEWMAN, PHYLLIS NOVIN, ANDREW PEPOY, RICK REESE, MIKE ROTE, SCOTT SHAW!, STEVE STEERE, JR., ART VILLANUEVA, MIKE WORLEY

Contributing Writers:
JAMES BATES, TERRY DELEGEANE, CHUCK DIXON, GEORGE GLADIR, EARL KRESS, ERIC ROGERS, SCOTT SHAW!, GAIL SIMONE, CHRIS YAMBAR

PRINTED IN CANADA

TABLE OF CONTENTS

SIMPSONS COMICS PRESENTS
BART SIMPSON
MENACE TO SOCIETY
#5
US $2.50
CAN $3.50

Z

MATT GROENING

WILD, WILD BART

GAIL "ANNIE OAKLEY" SIMONE SCRIPT	JOHN "JESSE JAMES" COSTANZA PENCILS	STEVE "BUTCH CASSIDY" STEERE, JR. INKS	LEE "SUNDANCE KID" LOUGHRIDGE COLORS	KAREN "CALAMITY JANE" BATES LETTERS	BILLY "THE KID" MORRISON EDITOR	MATT "BAT MASTERSON" GROENING BIG BOSS

PLOK!
PLOK!
PLOK!

DR. RALPH BRANELESS. MARTIMUS, I KNOW THAT EVIL GENIUS IS AT THE BOTTOM OF THIS!
WILD WEST AIR HOCKEY

MARTIMUS? WHY, I'M SURE I DON'T KNOW WHO YOU MEAN! I'M SHERRI, THE DANCE HALL GIRL WITH THE HEART OF GOLD!
Wild West
AIR HOCKEY

NICE TRY, MARTIMUS.

DASH IT ALL, BART. YOU ALWAYS SEE THROUGH MY CUNNING DISGUISES!

NO TIME TO PLAY DRESS-UP, MARTIMUS. BRANELESS IS STEALIN' ALL THE WATER OUT OF THE WEST. EVERY LAKE AND RIVER IS DRYIN' UP!

POP!
WITHOUT WATER, EVERY LIVING THING IN THE WEST IS IN DANGER!

PLOK!
VULCHERS GULCH
...AND THIS IS THE DIRTY, LOW-DOWN TOWN WHERE BRANELESS WAS LAST SEEN! SADDLE UP, MARTIMUS, WE'RE GOIN' RIDIN'!
A CAPITAL IDEA!

FASTER, MARTIMUS! PRESIDENT GRANT IS DEPENDIN' ON US!
I'M CHAFING BADLY, AND I'VE SWALLOWED A VARIETY OF INSECTS!

VULTURE'S GULCH SODA SALOON & GIN RUMMY PARLOR
WELL, THIS IS THE PLACE!
OH, I DO HOPE THEY HAVE PEPPERMINT JULEPS!
NO SHIRT, NO SHOES, NO SERVICE
OUTHOUSE FOR CUSTOMERS ONLY!

*ED'S NOTE: A CABALLERO IS A SPANISH HORSEMAN!–BUFFALO BILL MORRISON

OLD MAID
PLOK!
SMASH!
U.S. SECRET SERVICE
CHEWING GUM
DYNAMITE
FLAVOR!
CAUTION: NOT HYPERBOLE!
FLAVORED WITH REAL DYNAMIT
EXPLOSIVE!
(REALLY! WE MEAN IT

BLAM-AMMO!
WELL, NOW WE JUST HAVE TO WAKE ONE OF THEM UP, AND HE'LL TAKE US **RIGHT TO DR. BRANELESS!**
HOW **HUMILIATING!**

BART! **LOOK OUT!**

KONNK!
UGNNHH!

WELL, STRANGER, I GUESS YOU DIDN'T THINK THAT A **GIRL** MIGHT BE WORKING FOR BRANELESS, DID YOU? Y'ALL **SLEEP TIGHT**, NOW!
END PART ONE!

THERE ARE 29 MISTAKES IN THIS PICTURE! CAN YOU FIND THEM ALL?

1. THERE IS NO MINUTE HAND ON THE CLOCK. 2. GROUNDSKEEPER WILLIE IS WEARING TWO DIFFERENT TYPES OF SHOES. 3. THE LETTER "S" IS REVERSED ON THE BLACKBOARD. 4. THE NUMBERS 8 AND 9 ARE REVERSED ON THE CLOCK. 5. MEXICO IS SHOWN NORTH OF THE UNITED STATES ON THE GLOBE. 6. THE REMAINING 24 MISTAKES ARE ON BART'S TEST PAPER, ALTHOUGH HE DOESN'T KNOW IT YET!

SOLVE THE MYSTERY

HELP PRINCIPAL SKINNER FIND OUT WHO SPRAYED GRAFFITI ON THE CHALK BOARD.

ANSWER: LISA! SHE'S THE ONLY STUDENT WHO KNOWS THAT "I" COMES BEFORE "E" EXCEPT AFTER "C."

CONNECT THE DOTS PUZZLE

WHAT DO YOU GET WHEN YOU CONNECT ALL THE DOTS?

ANSWER: A COMIC BOOK THAT'S NO LONGER IN MINT CONDITION, SUCKER!

WILD, WILD BART
PART II

WAKING UP, CAPTAIN SIMPSON?
WHERE AM I? WHERE'S *MARTIMUS?*

OH, YOUR PARTNER. I WOULDN'T WORRY ABOUT HIM. HE ESCAPED, BUT WE'LL FIND HIM. AS FOR WHERE YOU ARE...WELL...

...I'D SAY YOU'RE IN A BIT OF *TROUBLE*, WOULDN'T YOU?

SO YOU'RE LETTIN' A GIRL DO ALL YOUR TALKIN' FOR YA, HUH, BRANELESS?
JESSICA SAYS I'M NOT SUPPOSED TO TALK MUCH. MY NAME IS RALPH. I HAD FLAPJACKS FOR BREAKFAST. I HAVE A ROCK IN MY SHOE. ROCKS TASTE BAD!

JEEZ, LADY, YOUR BOYFRIEND SOUNDS LIKE A REAL GENIUS!
HE'S NOT MY BOYFRIEND!

HE MAY NOT MAKE MUCH SENSE WHEN HE TALKS, BUT HE INVENTED THIS ELECTRICITY-PRODUCING MACHINE FOR ME, AND IT'S GOING TO CHANGE EVERYTHING!

WITH LIMITLESS ELECTRICITY, WE'LL SOON HAVE HAIR-DRYERS AND RADIOS AND COMPUTING MACHINES AND WHIRLPOOL BATHS AND TELEVISIONS! AND WITH TELEVISIONS, WE'LL HAVE...

...ANIMATED CARTOONS!

LADY, YOU'RE JUST AS CRAZY AS YOUR BOYFRIEND.
HE'S NOT MY BOYFRIEND!
DADDY SAYS "SPURS SHOULD STAY ON YOUR FEET!"

SO YOU SIPHONED OFF ALL THE WATER TO POWER THE MACHINE, HUH? VERY CLEVER.
YES, ISN'T IT? NOW... ANY LAST REQUESTS, CAPTAIN SIMPSON?

HERE'S MY CHANCE!
JUST ONE. GIVE ME BACK MY HAT!

OH, THAT. HERE YOU ARE...!
BUT YOU SAID I COULD BE A REAL COWBOY!

DID I FORGET TO MENTION THAT THE LAKE IS FILLED WITH PIRANHA?

ONCE NELSON PULLS THE LEVER TO START THE WATER WHEEL, YOU'LL GET TO MEET THEM PERSONALLY!
GOODBYE, CAPTAIN SIMPSON!
CHEW!
TEAR!
GNAW!
SNAP!
RIP!
REND!

HA, HA!
RRRCHKT!

GUESS IT WASN'T SO SMART TO KEEP MY LOCK PICKS IN MY HAT.
FORTUNATELY, MARTIMUS ALWAYS PUTS SOMETHIN' USEFUL IN THE HIDDEN COMPARTMENTS IN MY BOOT!

TAP!

D'OH!

TAP! TAP!
A BUBBLE WAND? MARTIMUS IS REALLY LOSING HIS EDGE, MAN!

PLEASE BE SOMETHING USEFUL THIS TIME!

TAP! TAP! TAP!
ACID
AN ACID-SHOOTING CANDY DISPENSER! WAY TO GO, MARTIMUS!

A FEW MINUTES AND FOUR MELTED LOCKS LATER...
OWWWWWWW!!!

THEY AREN'T GOING TO GET AWAY WITH THIS. "TELEVISION"..."ANIMATED CARTOONS"...THEY'RE BOTH **NUTS!**

HEY, MARTIMUS! I KNEW IT WAS YOU IN **DISGUISE** ALL ALONG! THAT FACE IS TOO **UGLY** TO BE REAL!
WHY DIDN'T YOU **SAVE** ME?

BAAM!!!

OKAY, SO YOU'RE **NOT** MARTIMUS. GROAN!
GET UP, HOMBRE, SO I CAN KNOCK YA **DOWN** AGAIN!

KEEP **LAUGHIN'**...

...**SUCKER!!!**
...HUH?

AAAAH!! THERE'S A **SHARK** IN MY BRITCHES! GET IT OUT! **GET IT OUT!!!**

THAT SOUNDS LIKE NELSON'S IN TROUBLE!
I JUST HAD AN IDEA FOR A VACUUM THAT CUTS HAIR!

GIVE IT UP, GIRLIE! YOU AND YOUR BOYFRIEND WILL NEVER ESCAPE!

HE'S NOT MY BOYFRIEND!!!
BAP!
WHEEEEE! I'M FLYING!

OW!!!
OW!
OW!
...OW, FLYING HURTS!

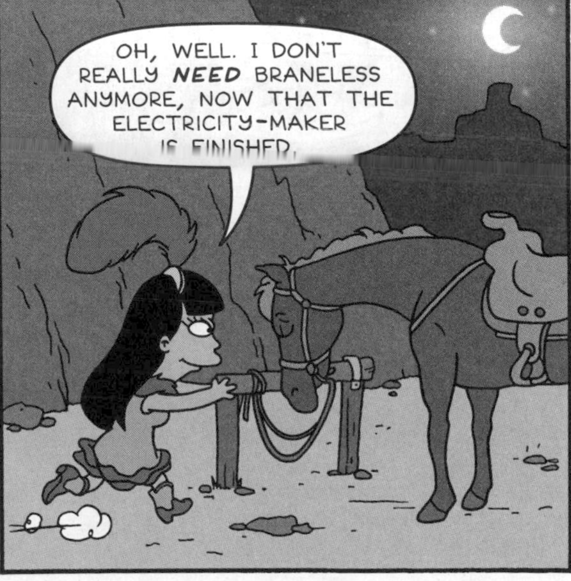
OH, WELL. I DON'T REALLY NEED BRANELESS ANYMORE, NOW THAT THE ELECTRICITY-MAKER IS FINISHED.

OH, YOU DON'T HAVE A HORSE, CAPTAIN? HOW SAD! GUESS I'LL JUST ESCAPE THEN! BYE, NOW!

NOT SO FAST, YOUNG LADY! MARTIMUS PRINCE, MASTER OF DISGUISE, AT YOUR SERVICE!
HE'S NOT MY...OH, NEVER MIND.
GOOD WORK, MARTIMUS! I GOT HER BOYFRIEND RIGHT HERE!
MY HEAD HAS MOUNTAINS!

SOON...
ANOTHER THREAT TO NATIONAL SECURITY DEFEATED, MARTIMUS, AND ALL THE WATER HAS BEEN RETURNED TO WHERE IT BELONGS!
YES. GOOD WORK, I SAY! "ANIMATED CARTOONS"...WHAT WAS THAT MADMAN THINKING?

I DON'T KNOW, BUT I'D SAY HE'S EASILY THE GREATEST CRIMINAL GENIUS THE WORLD HAS EVER KNOWN.

THAT DOGGIE HAS HORNS!
OH, SHUT UP!
THE LONESOME END!

WHEN WILL YOU ***HOOLIGANS*** LEARN THAT THE HALLS AND RECREATIONAL AREAS OF SPRINGFIELD ELEMENTARY ARE ***MY*** BEAT, AND ITS VERY INHABITANTS ARE ***MINE*** TO ***SERVE*** AND ***PROTECT*** FROM THE LIKES OF ***YOU!***

TOO BAD YOU'RE MISSING A BADGE, A GUN, A NIGHTSTICK, OR ANYTHING ELSE THAT COULD ***SCARE ME STRAIGHT!*** HA, HA!

BE THAT AS IT MAY, I HAVE ARRANGED A ***PERFECT PUNISHMENT*** FOR YOU!

THE CASE OF THE HANGING SHOES

FROM THE SECRET FILES OF LISA SIMPSON

TERRY DELEGEANE
SCRIPT

IGOR BARANKO
PENCILS AND INKS

ART VILLANUEVA
COLORS

KAREN BATES
LETTERS

MATT GROENING
SUPER SLEUTH

SO HE WONTS ME TO FETCH THESE ORTHOPEDIC SHOES FROM THE WIRES, DOES HE? AH'D LIKE TO FETCH HIM A FISTFUL OF WILLIE!

...WOT'S THIS, NOW? SOMETHING IS QUEER IN THE STATE OF EDINBURGH.

WILLIE, WHAT'S TAKING SO LONG TO GATHER THE EVIDENCE?
SOMEONE'S USED SOME HIGH-FALUTIN' ROPE TRICKERY TO TIE THESE SHOES TOGETHER.
I HAVEN'T BEEN WITNESS TO SUCH FINE KNOT WORK SINCE ME DAYS IN THE SCOTTISH NAVY.
WELL, CUT THE KNOT AND BRING IT HERE!

THAT'S IT!
SNAP!

?!
?!
A-HA! JUST AS I SUSPECTED. PRINCIPAL SKINNER, LET NELSON GO!
?!

NOW, LISA, GIVE ME BACK THAT KNOT THIS INSTANT!
BUT DON'T YOU SEE...

...THIS IS A *DUTCH CRINGLE* KNOT. IT IS A SPECIAL *KNOT* THAT'S USED TO FORM A HANDLE OR CONNECTION BETWEEN TWO POINTS OR OBJECTS.
ONLY THE *NIMBLEST* OF HANDS KNOWS HOW TO MAKE THIS KNOT AND HARDLY *ANYONE* IN SPRINGFIELD.

"IN FACT ONLY *ONE JUNIOR CAMPER* HAS EARNED A *SPECIAL MERIT BADGE* FOR HIS WAY AROUND A CORD OF TWINE..."

..*MARTIN PRINCE!*

LISA, THIS IS RIDICULOUS. CERTAINLY, YOU ARE NOT *ACCUSING* MARTIN PRINCE OF CONSTRUCTING AN *ELABORATE PLOT* TO FALSELY ACCUSE HIS WOULD BE *TORMENTOR*.

BUT IT'S *TRUE!* ALAS, I AM UNDONE. CHECK AND MATE, LISA. YOU MUST UNDERSTAND THAT MY ACTIONS WERE ONLY TO STAVE OFF MY FOE'S THREAT OF GIVING ME *"THE MOTHER OF ALL WEDGIES!"*

"AFTER BEING THREATENED WITHIN AN INCH OF MY LIFE BY NELSON, I DETERMINED TO BEST HIM AT HIS OWN GAME, TURNING THE PROVERBIAL TABLE ON MY ADVERSARY."
"I DEVISED A SCHEME TO SET-UP MY RIVAL FOR THE FALL OF HIS YOUNG LIFE."
BUT THAT DOESN'T EXPLAIN HOW A NOODLE-ARMED PANTY WAIST, SUCH AS YOU, WITH NARY THE STRENGTH OF A WEE BABE, WAS ABLE TO HEFT THOSE SHOES OVER THE POWER LINES.
"THAT'S SIMPLE. I MERELY BORROWED THE CATAPULT FROM MY PRIZE-WINNING, EXTRA CREDIT DISPLAY OF MEDIEVAL INSTRUMENTS OF WAR AND CALCULATED THE PRECISE TRAJECTORY. THEN, I RETURNED IT IN A TRICE, AND NO ONE WAS THE WISER."
I THINK I HAVE HEARD ABOUT ENOUGH. OFF WITH THE BOTH OF YOU! YOU TOO, BART!
BUT WAIT, PRINCIPAL SKINNER! NELSON ONLY THREATENED MARTIN, AND BART DIDN'T DO ANYTHING AT ALL!
IT'S ALL A MATTER OF TIME, LISA, AND BESIDES, MOTHER'S GARDEN NEEDS TENDING. THOSE HYDRANGEA BUSHES WON'T JUST PRUNE THEMSELVES. AND THEN THERE'S THE WEEDING AND THE SEEDING...
WHA-!
SIGH
EH!
THE END

BART SIMPSON'S DAY OFF
WIGGLE PUPPY LIKES YOUR LEG.
:SIGH:
C'MON, BART. WHERE ARE YOU?
JAMES BATES-SCRIPT
CAROLYN KELLY-PENCILS
SCOTT MCRAE-INKS
LEE LOUGHRIDGE-COLORS
KAREN BATES-LETTERS
BILL MORRISON-EDITOR
MATT GROENING-GRAND MARSHALL

YIKES!
YANK!

WHAT'S THE BIG IDEA?
SHHH!

IN JUST A FEW MOMENTS THE BUS WILL COME AND GO, AND WE'LL BE *FREE!*
FREE?

SMELL THAT FRESH AIR! LOOK AT THE BLUE SKY! IT'S TOO NICE A DAY TO *WASTE* AT SCHOOL. TODAY IS A DAY FOR *FUN*.

FORGET IT, BART. WE'LL GET *CAUGHT*.
NO, WE WON'T.

BUT TODAY IS THE *SPRINGFIELD TOURNAMENT OF POSIES!* WE'LL BE WATCHING THE PARADE AT SCHOOL AND WON'T EVEN *HAVE* CLASSES.
SCHOOL IS SCHOOL. WITH EVERYONE PAYING ATTENTION TO THE *STUPID PARADE,* NO ONE WILL NOTICE WE'RE *MISSING*.
THE DAY IS *OURS!*

JUST LOOK AT THOSE POOR SAPS! C'MON, MILHOUSE...

...I **GUARANTEE** IT'LL BE FUN. SO WHAT'S IT GONNA BE? **SCHOOL OR FUN**?

I CHOOSE **FUN**!
LET THE **PARTY** BEGIN.

ARF! ARF!

SOON...
I DON'T KNOW, BART. IS SITTING OUTSIDE THE KWIK-E-MART ALL THE FUN YOU HAD IN MIND?
NO...

OKAY. WHAT'S NEXT?
...HOW ABOUT ...A SQUISHEE RACE!

READY? GO!

SSLLUUUURRRRPP!

...AND BART SIMPSON REMAINS THE UNDEFEATED AND UNDISPUTED CHAMPION OF THE WORLD!
MY BRAIN! MY POOR, FROZEN BRAIN!

PLEASE MOVE YOUR FRIEND OR PLACE HIM IN THE TRASH RECEPTACLE PROVIDED.

THANKS, BART.

AYE, CARUMBA!
STUDENT DISCIPLINE WEEKLY
"BEHIND THE WOODSHED" NOSTALGIA ISSUE

OUCH! WHAT'S THE BIG IDEA?
IT'S SUPERINTENDENT CHALMER'S HENCHMAN, LEOPOLD!
OH NO, WE'RE SO DEAD!
CHIPS

HELLO, MR. LEOPOLD, SIR. ARE YOU WORKING AS A TRUANT OFFICER TODAY?
YEAH, BUT I'M JUST HERE FOR A CLAMATO JUICE.
OH, GOOD. MAY I ALSO INFORM YOU ABOUT THE TWO SCHOOL-AGED RAPSCALLIONS HIDING OUTSIDE?
BEAKLOAF 3 for $1.

COME BACK HERE, YOU LITTLE MAGGOTS! YOU CAN TRY TO RUN AND YOU CAN TRY TO HIDE, BUT YOUR BUTTS ARE MINE!

IS THIS YOUR IDEA OF FUN, BART?

VINTA
DID WE LOSE HIM?

VINTAGE CLOTHI
YANK!

AGE CL

EXCUSE ME. HAVE YOU SEEN TWO **WORTHLESS** LITTLE PUNKS RUNNING AROUND HERE?
AIN'T NO KIDS 'ROUND HERE, MAN.
UH, NO, WE DIDN'T SEE BART AND MILHOUSE.

HMM? OKAY. THANKS.
QUIET, YOU **NUMBSKULL**!

YOU ALMOST GOT US **CAUGHT**, MAN.
SORRY, I WAS **SCARED**.
JUST **RELAX** AND WE'LL GET OUT OF THIS.
BART, AM I **PRETTY**?

WHEN I FIND THOSE **TWERPS**, I'M GONNA TEAR 'EM A NEW PIE-HOLE.

OOF!
BURP!
WHUMP!

WHOA, **SONNY AND CHER**! MY HALLUCINATIONS ARE **IMPROVING**. I USUALLY SEE **THE CAPTAIN AND TENNILLE** AFTER I'VE BEEN TO MOE'S.

SPRINGFIELD TOURNAMENT OF POSIES PARADE

HOLD ON. I THINK WE'VE FINALLY LOST HIM.
I DON'T THINK SO. LOOK!

YOU WORMS ARE ABOUT TO BE PUT ON THE HOOK!

BART, I'M SCARED.
ME TOO! JUMP!

OW-OW-OW.
OOF!

NOW THOSE ARE SOME BIG ELEPHANT PATTIES!
YOU'RE THE EXPERT.

GRAMPA!
HEY, WEREN'T YOU TWO ON LAWRENCE WELK?
IT'S ME. BART!

I GOTCHA, BOY!

OH NO, HERE GOES MY NEW HIP.
BOINK!
WHEW! I'M LUCKY THAT MINI-CAR RUNS ON TWO AAA BATTERIES.

I GOT YOU, ABE.

YOU'RE TOAST! YOUR SHENANIGANS END HERE!
NO WAY, JOSÉ. YOU GOT NOTHIN' ON US.

NOTHIN'?

LOOK WHERE WE ARE. WE'RE AT SCHOOL, DUDE!
YEAH!
WE LOVE POSIES!

WELL, MILHOUSE, I THINK WE'VE HELPED MY GRAMPA ENOUGH.
BEING THE MASONS' **OFFICIAL** POSIES PARADE SONNY AND CHER IMPERSON-ATORS HAS BEEN AN HONOR WE WON'T SOON FORGET.
HUH?

NICE **DRESS,** MILHOUSE.
THANKS, MRS. KRABAPPEL.

I CAN'T BELIEVE WE MADE IT!
JUST ANOTHER **VICTORY** FOR THE BOY, THE MYTH, THE LEGEND, THEY CALL...

...**BART SIMPSON!** LEOPOLD TELLS ME HE SPOTTED YOU TWO AT THE KWIK-E-MART, WHICH IS **NOT** ON THE PARADE ROUTE! **YOU'RE BUSTED!**

AW, MAN! WE'VE GOT A WHOLE MONTH IN **DETENTION!**
YEAH, I'M SORRY. I'M PRETTY USED TO IT, BUT IT'S GONNA BE **ROUGH** ON YOU!
DON'T BE SORRY. I'VE NEVER HAD SO MUCH **FUN**.

IN FACT, I HAD **SO** MUCH FUN THAT I'M **CUTTING** SCHOOL **TOMORROW!**
AH, MILHOUSE...
NO, DON'T TRY TO TALK ME OUT OF IT!

I DON'T HAVE THE HEART TO TELL HIM TOMORROW'S **SATURDAY!**
THE END

COMICS
BONGO
GROUP
SIMPSONS COMICS PRESENTS
BART SIMPSON
HIGH FLYER
#6
US $2.50
CAN $3.50

©2001 BONGO ENTERTAINMENT, INC. THE SIMPSONS ©&TM TWENTIETH CENTURY FOX FILM CORPORATION. ALL RIGHTS RESERVED.

EXIT
WATCH YOUR STEP
WOO HOO!
HHOOOOOOOOOOOOOOOTTTTT!!!

EXIT
PLINK!

RUSTLE!
RUSTLE!

ERT!
ERT!

MOE'S
OH, NO YOU DON'T, YOU **MANGY STRAY!**

YOU'RE NOT BRINGING YOUR ***FILTHY GERMS*** INTO ***MY*** BAR, YOU ***DISGUSTING*** STREET BEAST!

MY HAIR ITCHES.
IT'S PROBABLY JUST YOUR ***HEAD LICE*** KICKING IN AGAIN, BARNEY. C'MON, WE'LL CLEAN YOU UP BACK IN THE KITCHEN.

TOSS!

?

GULP!

The Supercat of Springfield!

CHRIS YAMBAR	DAN DECARLO	MIKE DECARLO	ART VILLANUEVA	KAREN BATES	BILL MORRISON	MATT GROENING
STORY	LAYOUTS	PENCILS/INKS	COLORS	LETTERS	EDITOR	SOMETHING FUNNY

THE HORROR!
DON'T MAKE ME WATCH! ANYTHING BUT THIS!
OH, PLEASE. IT'S JUST THE NEWS!

NEWS SNOOZE! POLITICS THIS. HUMAN INTEREST THAT! BOOORING!

BUT WITHOUT THE NEWS, HOW WE WOULD GET AN UNBIASED PERSPECTIVE ON FILTHY COMMIES, TREE-HUGGING ENVIRONMENTALISTS, AND GUN-LOVING, RIGHT-WING EXTREMIST REPUBLICANS?
GOOD POINT, DAD!
OH, BROTHER!

THE BOY RESPECTS HIS OLD DAD, AND THAT'S ALL I COULD EVER ASK...
SHHH! DUMMY UP, HOMER! CHECK OUT THIS NEWS STORY.

SPRINGFIELD POLICE GOT A TIMELY ASSIST IN STOPPING A CARLOAD OF CROOKS EARLIER THIS AFTERNOON BY NONE OTHER THAN WHAT IS NOW BEING CALLED... THE SUPERCAT OF SPRINGFIELD.

WITH US NOW IS POLICE CHIEF WIGGUM WITH AN EYEWITNESS REPORT. WHAT CAN YOU TELL US ABOUT THIS SIGHTING, CHIEF?
UH....WE WERE IN HOT PURSUIT OF THE SHELBYVILLE THREE WHEN THIS CAT JUMPED IN FRONT OF THEIR CAR AND STOPPED THEM COLD.

THEN, THE SUPERCAT **FLEW AWAY** LIKE SOME KIND OF BEAUTIFUL, STREAKY-BLACK SNOWBALL. HE...HE TURNED AND **WINKED** AT ME, TOO. IT WAS VERY **SPECIAL**.
COOL!

OOH, PLEASE! WHAT'S NEXT? FLYING HORSES? A SUPER-POWERED MONKEY?
MASKED DOGS WHO LIVE WITH THEIR BILLIONAIRE MASTERS IN GIANT CAVES FILLED WITH BATS???!!

ANIMALS ARE JUST **MINDLESS CREATURES** WHO EXIST TO SERVE AND ENTERTAIN US. THEY CAN'T BE OUR SUPERIORS. THEY CAN'T JUST...

...

EXCUSE ME, CHILDREN! I MUST **OVERFEED** CAT NOW!

MUST GO TO STORE AND BUY **FRESH HALIBUT FILLETS** AND **SWORDFISH STEAKS** NOW! WILL RETURN SOON...

....OH, YES! AND I WILL BRING BACK **COMIC BOOKS** FOR **BRILLIANT** SON, BART, AND COPIES OF "TEEN STEAM" FOR **WONDERFUL** DAUGHTER, LISA, TOO!

SNOWBALL II!! YOU...YOU'RE...

YES, BART. OUR LITTLE SNOWBALL II IS **REALLY**...THE SUPERCAT OF SPRINGFIELD! I DON'T KNOW HOW THIS ALL HAPPENED, BUT ONE THING IS FOR CERTAIN...

...WE'RE THE **LUCKIEST KIDS IN TOWN!**

YOU KNOW WHAT THIS MEANS, DON'T YOU, BART?
YEAH! SNOWBALL II CAN DO ALL MY HOME-WORK!

EVEN **BETTER** THAN THAT.

"ON MONDAY, THE SUPERCAT OF SPRINGFIELD AND HER ***MYSTERIOUS SIDEKICKS*** FOILED FAT TONY D'AMICO'S PLAN TO STEAL ***SCRATCH-OFF LOTTERY TICKETS*** AND REPLACE THEM WITH ***SCRATCH AND SNIFFS!***"

"ON TUESDAY, THE SUPERCAT ***REIGNITED*** THE SPRINGFIELD TIRE YARD AFTER THE ***PERPETUALLY-BURNING LANDMARK*** WAS ***EXTINGUISHED*** BY ***MEDDLING ECOLOGISTS*** EARLIER IN THE WEEK."

"ON WEDNESDAY, THE SUPERCAT CONTRIBUTED ENTERTAINMENT TO THE INJURED DELIVERY PERSONS ASSOCIATION BY CHASING C. MONTGOMERY BURNS', USUALLY, BLOODTHIRSTY WATCHDOGS ALL OVER HIS ESTATE."

"ON THURSDAY, THE SUPERCAT GAVE ***FREE X-RAYS*** TO EVERY CITIZEN WHO VISITED THE KWIK-E-MART. OWNER APU NAHASAPEEMAPETILON WAS SO HAPPY WITH THE SALES FOR THE DAY, HE TOOK A ***HALF-HOUR VACATION***. THERE WERE 63 ***ARRESTS***."

WELCOME, ***DO-GOODERS!***
WELCOME TO MY ***SECRET HIDEOUT!***
I HOPE THE ***TRANSPORTER BEAM***
DIDN'T DISTRESS YOU...
THUMP!
WHUMP!

...BUT THAT IS ***MY JOB!!***
DR. COLOSSUS!!!

RELAX, CHILDREN. YOU'RE IN GOOD HANDS.
CLAP!
CLAP!

WHAT DO YOU WANT FROM US, YOU ***CRIMINAL CREEP?***
ACTUALLY, NOTHING FROM YOU TWO. I'M AFTER THE ***RAW POWER*** BEHIND YOUR KITTEN. LET ME EXPLAIN MY PLAN TO YOU.

I'VE BEEN LOOKING FOR A ***NEW POWER SOURCE*** FOR A SPECIAL PROJECT OF MINE, AND THEN I SAW YOUR SUPERCAT'S ***EXPLOITS*** ON TV.
WHEN I REALIZED THE ***POTENTIAL,*** I TRANSPORTED YOU ALL HERE.

DK 3000

SAY HELLO TO ***DESTRUCTO-KAT* 3000!**

SHUK!

I CAN'T GET LOOSE, LISA. I'M NOT STRONG ENOUGH.
WAIT A MINUTE, BART! LOOK!

BWA-HA-HA-HA!

WHAT IS GOING ON? YOU'RE NOT GOING TO...TO...

HAAACK!
KLANG!

HA! KNOCKED OUT BY A SUPER HAIRBALL!
SNOWBALL II! YOU DID IT! YOU SAVED SPRINGFIELD!

C'MON, LISA. LET'S GET OUTTA HERE AND LET THE COPS CLEAN UP THIS MESS!
I'M WITH YOU, BIG BROTHER. LET'S GO!

NOW, WHAT *IDIOT* WOULD GO AND LEAVE ONE OF THOSE *RADIOACTIVE THINGAMABOBS* LAYING AROUND LIKE THAT?!

I'LL BE BACK AGAIN, SPRINGFIELD, AND NEXT TIME I'LL *BRING YOU TO YOUR KNEES*!

SURE YOU WILL, FOUR EYES. SURE YOU WILL. IF *CHURCH* WON'T DO IT, THEN WHAT HOPE HAVE *YOU* GOT?

OHH! LOOKIT HOW CUTE YOU TWO LOOK DRESSED UP LIKE THEM *CRIME FIGHTERS* ON TV.

AH, THERE'S NOTHIN' LIKE A HALF-FULL ***TRASH DUMPSTER*** TO SPICE UP A ***BORING*** WALK TO SCHOOL!

WHOEVER THOUGHT AN ***EGGHEAD*** LIKE ***PROFESSOR FRINK*** WOULD HAVE A BUNCH OF ***COOL JUNK*** LIKE ***THIS***?

AND ***THIS*** IS JUST THE STUFF HE'S ***THROWN OUT!***

UNH, I DON'T THINK WE SHOULD BE ***MESSIN' AROUND*** BACK HERE, BART! THOSE ***CHEMICALS*** LOOK KINDA ***DANGEROUS!***

DO NOT PLAY ON OR AROUND
THANK YOU, FRINK LABORATORIES

BART SIMPSON AND MILHOUSE VAN HOUTEN IN:

"THE INVISIBLE NERD!"

SCRIPT AND PENCILS ***SCOTT SHAW!*** INKS ***TIM HARKINS*** COLORS ***RICK REESE*** LETTERS ***KAREN BATES*** EDITOR ***BILL MORRISON*** MISSING PERSON ***MATT GROENING***

I'VE BEEN HIT! I'M A GONER! MY ENTIRE SHORT LIFE SHOULD START FLASHING BEFORE MY EYES ANY MINUTE NOW!
DO NOT PLAY ON OR AROUND
THANK YOU, FRINK LABORATORIES

BUT I CAN'T SEE! YOU BLINDED ME WITH THAT STUFF, BART! BECAUSE OF YOU, I'M GONNA MISS MY OWN PRE-DEATH FLASHBACKS!

HMM, THIS IS THE PERFECT OPPORTUNITY TO LIVEN UP A BORING DAY...AND HAVE A LITTLE FUN AT OL' MILHOUSE'S EXPENSE, TOO! AH, THERE THEY ARE--JUST WHAT I WAS LOOKING FOR!

I'LL POCKET THESE EYEGLASSES THAT MILHOUSE DROPPED!

HAH! CHILDREN CAN BE SO CRUEL! AND I JUST HAPPEN TO BE AN OVERACHIEVER IN CHILDISH CRUELTY!

DON'T WORRY, MILHOUSE, OL' BUDDY, I'M HERE!
BUT UNHH-- MILHOUSE, WH-WHERE ARE YOU?
I'M RIGHT HERE, BART! OR DID THAT STUFF MAKE YOU BLIND, TOO?

WAIT A MINUTE... YOU CAN'T SEE ME?
B-BUT THEN, THAT WOULD MEAN--!

THAT'S RIGHT, MILHOUSE! PROFESSOR FRINK'S CHEMICALS MUST HAVE TRANSFORMED YOU TO BECOME (DARE I EVEN SAY IT?)--
PSST, I'M OVER HERE, BART!
--INVISIBLE TO THE HUMAN EYEBALL!!!

REALLY? YOU THINK SO?
NAHHH, IT CAN'T BE...

LOOK, MILHOUSE, AS ANY SELF-RESPECTING COMIC BOOK FAN KNOWS, DAREDEVIL GAINED HIS SENSORY SUPER-POWERS WHEN A RADIOACTIVE ISOTOPE ACCIDENTALLY BLINDED HIM!

NOW DO YOU BELIEVE THAT I REALLY, TRULY, CAN'T SEE YOU, MILHOUSE?
UH, I GUESS THAT MAKES SENSE, SINCE I CAN'T SEE ME, EITHER...BART, YOU'RE RIGHT--I CAN'T SEE A THING!!!

GOOD LORD! ⁝CHOKE!⁝ THERE'S NO OTHER EXPLANATION
--I AM INVISIBLE!!!

WELL, NOW THAT WE'VE ESTABLISHED THAT, ARE YOU READY TO REAP THE BENEFITS OF YOUR NEW-FOUND INVISIBILITY?
WHOA, YOU BET!
OH, THIS IS GONNA BE SO SWEET...
DO NOT PLAY ON OR AROUND
THANK YOU, FRINK LABORATORIES

UH, IT JUST OCCURRED TO ME, BART...IF I'M BLIND, JUST HOW AM I GONNA SEE THOSE "BENEFITS" YOU MENTIONED?

JUST STICK WITH ME, MILHOUSE! I'LL BE HAPPY TO PROVIDE A PLAY-BY-PLAY NARRATION DESCRIBING THE HILARIOUS HIJINKS THAT ARE BOUND TO ENSUE!

"HILARIOUS HIJINKS"? MAN, I SPEND WAY TOO MUCH TIME READING THE PROGRAM DESCRIPTIONS IN TV GUIDE.

THANKS, BART! YOU'RE A REAL PAL!
DON'T SWEAT IT, AMIGO! OUR FIRST SCHEDULED STOP WILL BE--

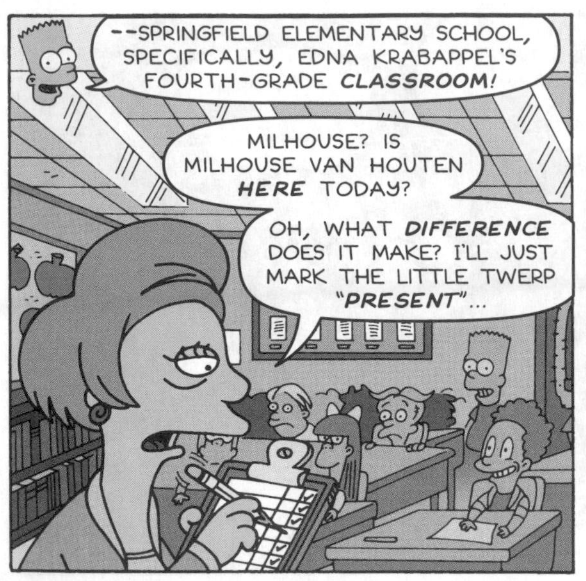
--SPRINGFIELD ELEMENTARY SCHOOL, SPECIFICALLY, EDNA KRABAPPEL'S FOURTH-GRADE CLASSROOM!
MILHOUSE? IS MILHOUSE VAN HOUTEN HERE TODAY?
OH, WHAT DIFFERENCE DOES IT MAKE? I'LL JUST MARK THE LITTLE TWERP "PRESENT"...

WHAT DID I TELL YOU, MILHOUSE?
WHOA, I REALLY AM INVISIBLE!

NEXT, THE SPRINGFIELD ELEMENTARY SCHOOL CAFETERIA, A PLACE JUST BEGGING FOR YOUR MISCHIEVOUS TOUCH, O INVISIBLE ONE!
WATCH ME FREAK OUT LUNCH LADY DORIS.
I AM THE GHOST OF ALL THE MYSTERY MEAT YOU SERVED LAST SEMESTER! YOU WILL BE PUNISHED FOR YOUR CRIMES!

HEY, CAN WE GET A MOP OVER HERE?
LOOK OUT, MILHOUSE, YOU KNOW THIS CAFETERIA HAS A STRICT "NO TIPPING" POLICY!
SPLORK!
WOW, SHE WAS SO SCARED, SHE ALMOST DROPPED HER SERVING-SCOOP!

PROFESSOR VON SIMPSON'S HYGIENE CLASS IS NOW IN SESSION!
GREETINGS, LADIES! IT IS I, THE INVISIBLE PHANTOM OF THE LAVATORY! BWOOOHAHAHAH!!!

EEEEEEEEEEEEEEEE!!!
ARGHH! LOOK OUT! YOU'RE TRAMPLING ME!
YOU MAY BE INVISIBLE, MILHOUSE, BUT YOU SURE AIN'T INVULNERABLE!
STAMPEDE!

WHAT SAY WE TAKE A TRIP TO THE ANDROID'S DUNGEON FOR SOME "FREE" READING...
PSST, MILHOUSE, HOW ABOUT TAKING THAT BOX OF OLD COMICS! WE CAN READ 'EM AND BRING 'EM BACK, AND NO ONE WILL KNOW!
UH, I DUNNO, BART...ISN'T THAT KINDA LIKE STEALING?

TELL YOUR FRIEND THAT I APPRECIATE HIM HAULING AWAY THOSE OLD COMICS! THEIR LAST OWNER HAD THE CHICKEN POX, AND NOW THEY'RE TOO INFECTIOUS TO SELL TO ANYONE!
PANT! WHEEZE! PUFF!
RICHIE
YEAH, I'LL GIVE HIM THE WORD...
...EVENTUALLY!

A BOY NEEDS TO BE NURTURED, EVEN AN INVISIBLE BOY! AND WHAT COULD BE MORE NURTURING THAN YOUR VERY OWN HOME-SWEET-HOME?
AND SO THEN I TOLD THAT GOOD-FOR NOTHING, DEAD-BEAT DAD, EX-HUSBAND OF MINE...
UH, MOM? HI, MOM! I BET YOU'RE WONDERING WHY YOU CAN'T SEE ME, HUH, MOM? MOM? MOMMY?!?

MILHOUSE, DOES YOUR MOM HAVE "CALL-WAITING" ON HER PHONE?
UH, YEAH, I THINK SO!
MAYBE YOU SHOULD JUST CALL HER ON THAT CELL PHONE AN' TELL HER YOU'RE INVISIBLE?!
NO, SHE NEVER ACCEPTS MY CALLS...

AND FINALLY, WE ASK THE QUESTION: WHAT'S A DAY WITHOUT A BIT OF MULTICULTURAL NIGHTLIFE?
I URGE YOU, PLEASE, KEEP YOUR HANDS WITHIN VIEW AT ALL TIMES, YOU MERRY YOUNG TRICKSTER!
NO PROBLEMO, APU! I'M AS INNOCENT AS THE DRIVEN SNOW CONES!
GRGLGRGLGRGLLL
SPEAKING OF WHICH... AIEEEE!
GIVE
GIVE

COME BACK HERE, YOU YOUNG RUFFIANS! I'LL GIVE YOU A FREE TASTE--OF MY STRAIGHT-FROM-THE-SPIGOT JAIPOORIAN JUSTICE!
I DON'T GET IT, BART! YOU SAID I'D BE ABLE TO DRINK ALL THE MANGO-CHUTNEY SQUISHEES I COULD HOLD, BUT APU BUSTED ME RED-HANDED!
UH, SORRY, MILHOUSE! I GUESS YOUR INVISIBILITY CAN BE TEMPORARILY CANCELLED OUT BY A MASSIVE "BRAIN-FREEZE"!

THE NEXT DAY...
WHAT'S WITH THE WACKY GET-UP, O INVISIBLE ONE?
WHEN SPRINGFIELD'S CITIZENRY SEES THIS STUFF MYSTERIOUSLY FLOATING IN MID-AIR, THEY'LL GO NUTSOID! IT'LL BE BIG LAUGHS, BART!
MILHOUSE, DO YOU HAVE MY FUR COAT? IT'S GENUINE "CUBIC MINKONIUM"!

OH, WE'RE GONNA GET SOME BIG LAUGHS, ALL RIGHT!
SUCKER!

BEFORE LONG...
OH, NO, LOOK WHO'S COMING THIS WAY!
UH, THAT'S REAL EASY FOR YOU TO SAY, BART...
GRUMBLE MUMBLE!

SNORT!
IT'S JIMBO, DOLPH AND KEARNEY!
GRUNT!
OBOY! BULLIES AHOY!
SNUK!

IT'S PAYBACK TIME FOR THE "INVISIBLE AVENGER"! HEY, DUDES! AM I BLOWING YOUR MINDS YET?
HONK!
HOOOOOOONNK!
I WAS AFRAID THIS MIGHT HAPPEN...

WHAT'S WITH FOUR-EYES HERE?
MAYBE HE'S BEEN GUZZLING TOO MANY BUZZ COLAS?
WHATEVER THE REASON, I THINK WE OUGHTA POUND THIS WEIRDO...
...JUST ON GENERAL PRINCIPLES, Y'KNOW?
HONK!
HOOOOOONNK!

MEANWHILE, BART'S EXPERIENCING A SURPRISING CRISIS-OF-CONSCIENCE...
SO, WHAT SHOULD I DO, GUYS?
POOF!
POOF!

BART, STEP IN BEFORE THOSE HOODS MAKE LUNCHMEAT OUT OF MILHOUSE!

BART, BEAT YER FEET OUTTA HERE AND SAVE YOUR OWN YELLOW HIDE, CHUM!

C'MON, YOU CUTE LI'L CARTOON CLICHÉS, I NEED A STRAIGHT ANSWER--
--NOW!

WELL, SO MUCH FOR MY BEING REASONABLE. IT'S TIME TO USE THE DIRECT APPROACH!
HI!! YAHHH!
PLUCK!
ARGHH!!!! I'M HIT!
SHUUUNNK!

SOMEHOW IT FIGURES THAT MY CONSCIENCE WOULD HAVE SUCH EXTREME MOOD-SWINGS!
THWUMP!

I HOPE YOU'VE RETURNED ALL YOUR LIBRARY BOOKS ON TIME, YOU LITTLE MOLE RAT!
YEAH, 'CAUSE YOU WON'T BE LEAVIN' YOUR HOSPITAL BED ANY TIME SOON!
WELL, I'M PRETTY SURE THAT ONE OF US IS, AND IT AIN'T ME!
THEN AGAIN, MAYBE I'M NOT INVISIBLE, AND YOU'RE JUST LOSING YOUR MINDS!?!
EXCUSE ME, GUYS, BUT I DON'T THINK YOU REALLY WANT TO CLOBBER MY FRIEND HERE!
SKIDDD!!!

WE DON'T? WHY TH' HECK NOT?
WELL, HE'S INVISIBLE.
HE AIN'T INVISIBLE!
SURE HE IS. I'LL PROVE IT!

OKAY, DUDE, PROVE IT NOW!
WELLLLL, LOOK AT IT THIS WAY...

...YOU CAN'T SEE GAS, BUT IT CAN POISON YOU, RIGHT?
YOU CAN'T SEE RADIATION, BUT IT CAN BURN YOU, RIGHT?
YOU CAN'T SEE GERMS, BUT THEY CAN MAKE YOU SICK, RIGHT?

WELL, IF SOMETHING INVISIBLE THAT YOU CAN'T SEE CAN DO ALL THAT TO YOU... ...JUST IMAGINE WHAT SOME-THING INVISIBLE THAT YOU CAN SEE WILL DO TO YOU!

LET'S GET OUTTA HERE!* HE'S USIN' CONTRADICTORY LOGIC!
SO WHY ARE WE RUNNIN'? THAT INVISIBILITY ACT OF HIS AIN'T CONVINCING!
WHO CARES, DUDE? HE SURE CONVINCED ME HE'S DANGEROUS AS ALL GET-OUT!!!
WELL, I GUESS THE "INVISIBLE AVENGER" SHOWED THEM!
PHEW!
*MANDATORY "BAD GUY" DIALOGUE

HEY, I CAN SEE AGAIN!
AND I CAN SEE MYSELF AGAIN, TOO!
YEAH, PROFESSOR FRINK'S CHEMICAL FORMULA MUST'VE FINALLY WORN OFF!

WAKKA-DING-HOY! DID SOMEONE MENTION MY NAME?
YOU BOYS WILL HAVE TO EXCUSE ME, BUT I'M LATE FOR MY WATER-SKIING LESSON! VOIVEL!
AY-YI-YIKES!!
AHOOOGAHHH!
THE END!

"24 HOURS IN THE LIFE OF RALPH WIGGUM!"

SCRIPT AND PENCIL ART BY **SCOTT SHAW!** INKED BY **SCOTT MCRAE** COLORED BY **RICK REESE** LETTERED BY **KAREN BATES** EDITED BY **BILL MORRISON** ENCOURAGED BY **MATT GROENING**

"RALPH WIGGUM" CREATED BY CLANCY AND SARA WIGGUM

7:37 AM
OOH... SHINY!

7:49 AM
WHEEE! I'M A FLYING SAUCER! ZOOM!
MR. KITTY-CAT, TAKE ME TO YOUR LEADER-- GARFIELD!

8:02 AM
HEY, I LIKE TO DIG, TOO!
YEAH, KID, I CAN SEE THAT! NOW WOULD YOU STOP DIGGIN'? PLEASE?
PICK!
PICK!
ECHHH...

8:14 AM
SUPERFLY GLUE-WORKS
"WE REALLY STICK IT TO THE MAN"
SNIFF! SNIFF!
MMMM...IT SMELLS NICE, LIKE OLD HORSIES!

8:23 AM
COMING SOON
THE REVENGE OF THE MONSTER THAT DEVOURED
CIRC' DE PRETENTIO
FEATURING A VERY SPECIAL GREASEPAINT TRIBUTE TO JERRY LEWIS!
BOY-OH-BOY! in concert!
47 DIFFERENT BOY BANDS!!!
ASAURUS IS BACK!!!
SPORTS ARENA!!!
POST NO BILLS
DON'T MISS THE RED SLUSH TOUR OF ITCHY AND SCRATCHY ON ICE!
RIDE CHUNK-BLOWER!!!
NOW AT SPRINGFIELD'S NEWEST THEME PARK,
WHIPLASH ACRES
NEAT-O KEEN-O!
BUT MY NAME'S NOT "BILL"...

8:30 AM
HI, LISA! OFFICER PUPPY AND I HAD DONUTS FOR BREAKFAST!
UH, DON'T LOOK NOW, RALPH...
...BUT I THINK YOU'VE STILL GOT A BIG ONE AROUND YOUR NECK!
BRRRRRRINNNNNGGGG!!!

8:57 AM
IF TRAIN "A" IS TRAVELING 247 MILES AT 48 MILES AN HOUR AND TRAIN "B" IS TRAVELING 342 MILES AT 63 MILES AN HOUR, WHICH ONE WILL REACH THEIR MUTUAL DESTINATION FIRST?
RALPH, CAN YOU TELL US THE ANSWER TO THIS MATH PROBLEM?
SPELLING QUIZ TOMORROW!
BUT I LIKE BOTH CHOO-CHOOS!

9:32 AM
CLASS, CAN EACH OF YOU FIND WHERE YOU LIVE?
:SIGH!: VERY ACCURATE, RALPH.
CITY OF SPRINGFIELD
EARTH'S MOON

10:43 AM
OOH, GOODY! I GET TO PLAY CENTER POSITION!
BUT ISN'T DODGE-BALL PLAYED WITH ONLY ONE BALL?

11:22 AM
MISS HOOVER, IS THIS A GOOD GRADE OR A BAD GRADE?
:SIGH!: RALPH, YOUR GUESS IS AS GOOD AS MINE.

12:47 PM
OOH, WHO WANTS TO TRADE LUNCHES?
LET'S SEE, I'VE GOT A BOLOGNA SANDWICH, A BAG OF CORN CHIPS, AND AN APPLE!
WELL, I'VE GOT A TUNA FISH SAND-WICH, CELERY STICKS WITH PEANUT BUTTER, AND A BANANA!
NUMMY-NUMS! I'VE GOT A JAR OF PASTE!

2:31 PM
WOW, JUST LISTEN TO RALPH SNORE!
ZZZZZZZZZZZ
YEAH, HE'S REALLY SAWING LOGS!

3:05 PM
BRRRRRRRINNNNNGGGG!!!
MY BRAIN HURTS!

3:12 PM
?
THIS DOGGIE WAS MY FAVORITE CARTOON CHARACTER!
JIGGA JIGGA JIGGA JIGGA
RIDE POOCHIE!
BUT HE DIED ON THE WAY BACK TO HIS HOME PLANET!

3:28 PM
THANKS, KID, BUT I REALLY DON'T NEED ANY HELP! NOW HURRY ALONG! I'VE GOTTA GET THIS THING FINISHED BY TONIGHT, OR ELSE THE CLIENT'S GONNA KICK MY BUHHH---?!?
MISTER, I PAINT WHAT I SEE!
SLAP! SLAP!
SPRINGFIELD SAVINGS

4:07 PM
AND TO THINK THAT I SAW IT ON...
HEY, WHAT STREET IS THIS, ANYWAY?
MULBERRY STREET

4:19 PM
LITTERS O' CRITTERS
PET SHOP
HI, MISTER, I'M JUST VISITING GOLDIE! HE'S THE ONE WHO LOOKS LIKE FONZIE, ONLY TALLER!
ED

4:31 PM
DINGDINGDING!
CLANG!
SPRINGFIELD VIDEO ARCADE
BLEEP!
DOINK!
BLOOP!
VROOP!
GIGGLE!
THIS IS THE BESTEST VIDEO GAME EVER!
TRICKLE!

4:46 PM
DO *I* LIVE HERE?
IF I **DON'T**, THAT DOGGIE LOOKS **AWFULLY** FAMILIAR!
GROAN!
LARD LAD DONUTS

5:53 PM
SIGH!
GOLDIE FUND
FISH FOOD
SPRINKLE!

6:15 PM
GOSH, HOMEWORK IS **HARD**!
EVEN **HARDER** THAN REMEMBERING TO **BREATHE**!

6:57 PM
SO, HONEY, WHAT HAPPENED TO **YOU** TODAY?
OH, NOTHIN' **SPECIAL**, MOMMY...
GOOD...**PASS** ME THEM **PORK CHOPS**, WILL YA?

7:22 PM
AND **NOW**, BACK TO OUR REGULAR PROGRAMMING HERE ON THE **CAR-CHASE NETWORK**...
DADDY, CAN'T WE WATCH THE **CARTOON CHANNEL** FOR A WHILE?
NAHH, THOSE "**ROADRUNNER**" **CARTOONS** ALWAYS **DEPRESS** ME! THEY'VE GOT LOTSA **PURSUITS**, BUT THAT **GOOD-GUY COYOTE** ALWAYS GETS **CLOBBERED**!
Y'KNOW, I REALLY **HATE** THAT STINKIN' BIRD!

8:24 PM
LOOK, DUCKIE, I'M **SHRIVELING** INTO A BIG OL' **PRUNE**!
UH-OH! I HOPE DADDY DOESN'T PUT ME IN A **DANISH PASTRY**!
SPLISH!
SPLASH!

8:42 PM
OOOH, I ALWAYS FORGET. WHICH HOLE DOES MY HEAD GO THROUGH?

8:53 PM
WELL, SWEET DREAMS MY LITTLE CITIZEN! DON'T LET THE BEDBUGS BITE!
SMEK!
OH, THESE AREN'T BEDBUG BITES, DADDY! THESE BITES ARE FROM DEER TICKS!

9:06 PM
CLAP ON, CLAP OFF, CLAP ON, CLAP OFF--
CLAP! CLAP!

9:07 PM
CLICK!
PLOP!
ZZZZZZZZ

⁝WHIMPER!⁝...MAKE IT...⁝MUMBLE⁝...STOP... ⁝WHIMPER!⁝

6:14 AM
SPRINGFIELD
OHHH, WHAT A NIGHTMARE!
NEVER THE END!

BONGO COMICS GROUP
SIMPSONS COMICS PRESENTS
BART SIMPSON
BOY OF MYSTERY
#7
US $2.50
CAN $3.50
MATT GROENING
Free Donuts

CHRIS YAMBAR STORY
DAN DECARLO LAYOUTS
LUIS ESCOBAR PENCILS
MIKE ROTE INKS
RICK REESE COLORS
KAREN BATES LETTERS
MATT GROENING SEWER INSPECTOR

THE SPONSOR OF THIS YEAR'S FAIR IS THE OWNER OF THE ANDROIDS DUNGEON, WHO WOULD LIKE TO EXPLAIN...
SILENCE, EARTHLING! ALLOW ME TO INSTRUCT THE MICRO-MINIONS SEATED BEFORE US!

OOOF!
WHUMP!

HARKEN TO MY WORDS, CHILDREN OF THE ATOM! THREE OF YOU WILL BE REWARDED FOR YOUR EFFORTS TO EXALT SCIENCE THROUGH EXPERIMENTATION!
THE REST OF YOU WILL FEEL THE VICIOUS STING OF FAILURE AND CARRY IT ON INTO ADULT LIFE.

BEFORE THERE WAS A PRIMORDIAL OOZE FOR YOU TO CLIMB OUT OF--THERE WAS SCIENCE! BEFORE THE FIRST ROMULAN EVER APPEARED ON NETWORK TELEVISION--THERE WAS SCIENCE! BEFORE THE FIRST SQUISHEE WAS EVER DISPENSED AND SOLD WITH A MICROWAVED BURRITO--THERE WAS SCIENCE!

VERILY, IT WAS SCIENCE THAT GAVE US THE HOLOGRAPHIC TRADING CARD, THE BASIS FOR SCIENCE FICTION STORIES, AND THE DEEP DISH PIZZA...AND VERILY I SAY THAT IT WILL BE YOUR SCIENTIFIC EXPERIMENT WHICH WILL DETERMINE WHETHER OR NOT YOU WILL WIN ONE OF THREE SHOPPING SPREES AT THE ANDROIDS DUNGEON VALUED AT $25 EACH!

YOU ARE DISMISSED. GO TO YOUR BUSES, CHILDREN. PLEASE WALK, DON'T--
RUN! ARISE, FOR YOUR ESCAPE PODS HAVE ARRIVED! IT IS TIME TO RETURN TO YOUR NATIVE HOMEWORLDS! ***GO! FLEE!***

THAT MAN IS A ***RAVING LUNATIC!*** WHO IN THEIR ***RIGHT MIND*** WOULD LISTEN TO SUCH...

...***INSANITY***?
AND NOW, I TAKE MY LEAVE TO EXPLORE ***NEW HORIZONS*** AT THE NEIGHBORING ***TACO MAT***. GOOD DAY, SIR.

ONE WEEK LATER...
...NOW, IF I CAN ONLY ISOLATE THE PROPER...
GLAH WOOOSHA!

GAH! I CAN'T EVEN THINK WITH ALL THIS NOISE!
GLAH WOOOSHA!

CAN'T YOU GO SOMEWHERE ELSE? I'M TRYING TO...
GLAH WOOOSHA!

WHAT IN THE WORLD ARE YOU DOING, BART?!?

I'M FLUSHING BABY ALLIGATORS DOWN THE TOILET. WHAT ARE YOU DOING?
DANGER: CONTAINS BABY ALLIGATORS

I'M TELLING MOM!
GOODBYE #52. MAKE ME PROUD.
DANGER: CONTAINS BABY ALLIGATORS
GLAH WOOOSHA!

RELAX, LISA. REMEMBER WHEN WE GOT MONEY FROM DAD FOR OUR SCIENCE PROJECTS? YOU WENT OUT AND BOUGHT YOUR STUFF AT NERDS 'R' US, AND I WENT TO THE PET SHOP!
WHAT DO YOU MEAN? I DON'T SEE ANY SCIENCE PROJECT!

THAT'S THE BEAUTY OF IT, LIS. IT'S A SCIENCE PROJECT THAT DOES ITS OWN WORK. PLUS, NOBODY CAN COPY IT. MY EXPERIMENT IS COMPLETELY SAFE FROM PRYING EYES.
I'M A CINCH TO WIN FIRST PRIZE!
I'M AFRAID I DON'T UNDERSTAND.

WELCOME TO MY SECRET LABORATORY! THIS IS WHERE I AM DEFYING THE LAWS OF NATURE TO CREATE A NEW LIFE FORM! RIGHT UNDER THE UNSUSPECTING FEET OF THE PEOPLE OF SPRINGFIELD.

AND I OWE IT ALL TO DAD'S BOSS.
MR. BURNS?!

REMEMBER WHEN WE CAUGHT THAT *THREE-EYED MUTANT FISH*? MR. BURNS *CREATED* THAT FISH WHEN HE DUMPED *RADIOACTIVE WASTE* INTO OUR RIVER.
PEOPLE WERE SURE MAD ABOUT THAT.

SO WHY DO YOU THINK HE *REBUILT* THE ENTIRE *SEWAGE SYSTEM* FOR SPRINGFIELD?
SO WE'D HAVE *SAFER, CLEANER WATER*?

NO WAY! HE NEEDED A NEW PLACE TO GET RID OF HIS *RADIOACTIVE WASTE!*

SO COMBINE THAT FACT WITH THE BABY ALLIGATORS, AND WHAT DO YOU HAVE?
AN IDIOT FOR A BROTHER.

THREE MONTHS FROM NOW I'LL UNLEASH MY *ARMY OF GIANT, THREE-EYED, MUTANT ALLIGATOR MEN!* THAT SHOPPING SPREE AT THE ANDROIDS DUNGEON IS AS GOOD AS *MINE!*
I MEANT TO SAY, A *TOTAL* IDIOT FOR A BROTHER! THERE'S NO RADIOACTIVE WASTE IN THAT SEWER! THAT FISH WAS A *FLUKE!*

THREE MONTHS LATER...

EUREKA! I'VE ***GOT*** IT!

PHEW! I'M AFRAID TO ASK WHAT YOU ***DID*** IN HERE, LISA. THIS ROOM SMELLS LIKE...

...ROTTEN EGGS!
THE KIND OF ROTTEN EGGS THAT WILL BE ALL OVER YOUR FACE WHEN WE SHOW OUR EXPERIMENTS TOMORROW AT THE SCIENCE FAIR. HA!

SO WHAT KIND OF RESULTS DID YOU GET, DR. STINKYPANTS?
IF YOU MUST KNOW, I'VE BEEN ABLE TO ISOLATE A LONE AMINO ACID THAT COULD HOLD THE CURE TO THE COMMON COLD!

BY TAKING THESE EGGS, AND EXTRACTING THE PROPER AMOUNT OF AMINO ACID FROM THE DNA STRAND WHILE EXPOSING IT TO HARD LIGHT...
BLAH, BLAH, BLAH! EGG SALAD SANDWICHES FOR EVERYONE ON THE PLANET. WHO CARES? HURRY UP, LISA. IT'S TIME TO CHECK OUT MY EXPERIMENT!
DO NOT EAT
GLUE

LOOK OUT, SPRINGFIELD! HERE COMES BART SIMPSON AND HIS MUTANT ALLIGATOR MEN REVIEW! WOO-HOO!

UNNNGGH! MAN, IS THIS THING SEALED TIGHT! IT WOULD TAKE AN ARMY TO REMOVE THIS.
OR THE FLICK OF A LASER BEAM HYDRAULIC CODE DESCRAMBLER BUTTON.

I'VE BEEN MONITORING YOUR LITTLE EXPERIMENT, BART, AND HAVE COME TO SEE WHAT WE'VE CREATED FIRSTHAND.
MR. BURNS!!!
WHAT DO YOU MEAN, 'WHAT WE'VE CREATED'?!?

YOUR EXPERIMENT WAS CONDUCTED IN MY SEWER SYSTEM WITHOUT MY PERMISSION. SO, IF THERE ARE ANY MUTANT ALLIGATOR MEN UNDER THIS CITY, THEN I HAVE A RIGHT TO THEM, TOO.
ACCORDING TO OUR INTERPRETATION OF THE LAW, WHAT MR. BURNS SAYS IS PERFECTLY TRUE AND LEGAL.

I'LL BE THE JUDGE OF THAT!
CHIEF WIGGUM! WOW! I NEVER THOUGHT I'D BE HAPPY TO SEE YOU!
OKAY, MR. BURNS. LET'S POP THE TOP OFF THIS CAPER!

OHHH, ALL RIGHT. OPEN THAT MANHOLE FOR ME, SMITHERS, AND LET'S GET THIS OVER WITH!
YES, SIR!
CLICK!

PHEW! WHAT A HORRIBLE SMELL! OKAY, PEOPLE, WHO GOES DOWN FIRST? WHO'S MOST EXPENDABLE?

VERY FUNNY. OKAY, I'LL GO, BUT AFTER THE KIDS.
STILL HAPPY TO SEE HIM, BART?

I'LL SAY. I'VE GOT GUM ON MY SHOE.
THIS IS SO GROSS!
KEEP YOUR EYES OPEN. THERE COULD BE MUTANT GATORS LURKING ANYWHERE.

GASP! BART WAS RIGHT! THIS SEWER SYSTEM IS FILLED WITH RADIOACTIVE WASTE FROM THE NUCLEAR POWER PLANT!
CHIEF WIGGUM, YOU'VE GOT TO DO SOMETHING!

KEEP KICKING, CHIEF WIGGUM. ALLIGATORS LIKE BITING BARE FEET.
HERE, GATOR, GATOR, GATOR. COME TO PAPA.

SEAL IT BACK UP, BOYS. THERE'S NOTHING DOWN THERE TO **THREATEN** THE PEOPLE OF SPRINGFIELD. OUR WORK HERE IS **DONE**.
NO MUTANT ALLIGATOR MEN. PHOOEY! ALL THAT WORK FOR **NOTHING**.

OH, AND DON'T BE LATE AGAIN WITH YOUR DONATION TO THE **POLICE BENEVOLENCE FUND,** MR. BURNS.
BUT WHAT ABOUT THE **NUCLEAR WASTE?** BURNS SHOULD BE **ARRESTED!**
QUIET, LITTLE GIRL!
I STAND CORRECTED. THANK YOU, CHIEF WIGGUM.

THE NEXT DAY...
...THAT **CONCLUDES** OUR STUDENT SCIENCE EXHIBITION EXCEPT FOR BART SIMPSON, WHOSE "RADIOACTIVE ALLIGATOR MEN IN THE SEWER" EXPERIMENT **FAILED** TO SHOW RESULTS, AND LISA SIMPSON, WHOSE **ILLITERATE** FATHER ATE HER "EGGS FOR A COLD-FREE WORLD" EXPERIMENT.

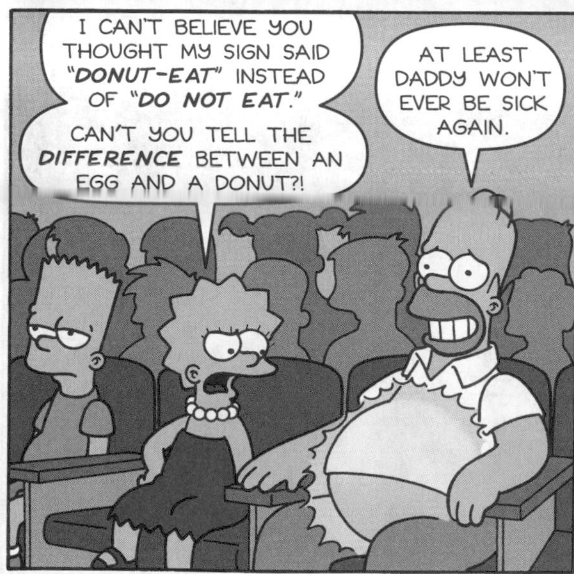
I CAN'T BELIEVE YOU THOUGHT MY SIGN SAID "**DONUT-EAT**" INSTEAD OF "**DO NOT EAT**."
CAN'T YOU TELL THE **DIFFERENCE** BETWEEN AN EGG AND A DONUT?!
AT LEAST DADDY WON'T EVER BE SICK AGAIN.

AND HERE TO PRESENT THIS YEAR'S AWARDS IS THE OWNER OF THE ANDROIDS DUNGEON.

BEHOLD! I HOLD IN MY HAND ENVELOPES CONTAINING THREE $25 SHOPPING SPREES AT THE ANDROIDS DUNGEON.
SINCE I ALONE WILL CHOOSE THIS YEAR'S WINNERS, I WILL DO SO ACCORDING TO MY OWN LAWS AND SUPERIOR REASONING.

...THIRD PLACE GOES TO RALPH WIGGUM FOR HIS "MY DAD'S SHOE IS STUCK TO MY HEAD WITH GUM" EXPERIMENT. I HAVEN'T SEEN ANYTHING SO FUNNY SINCE SPOCK LAUGHED OUT LOUD IN THE SECOND "STAR TREK" MOVIE.
THANKS, MISTER. THE SHOE KEEPS MY HEAD FROM WEARING A SKI CAP!

SECOND PLACE GOES TO LISA SIMPSON BECAUSE OF HER DISREGARD FOR THE CHOLESTEROL LEVEL OF HER EXPERIMENT AND BECAUSE SHE WILL PROBABLY SPEND HER $25 ON ALL THE GIRL-FRIENDLY COMICS I HAVE GATHERING DUST IN MY SHOP.
SCIENCE FAIR–
SPONSORED BY THE ANDROIDS DUNGEON
...BUT...
OH, LISA, I'M SO PROUD, MY ARTERIES FEEL LIKE FLUBBER.

AND FIRST PLACE GOES TO BART SIMPSON FOR FOLLOWING HIS DREAM TO CREATE A NEW RACE OF SUBTERRANEAN MUTANTS REGARDLESS OF THE DANGERS TO MANKIND AND SUPERHERO-KIND ALIKE.

HURRY, HOMER! WE'VE GOT AN ANGRY MOB ON OUR HANDS!
SMAK!
MY KID SHOULD HAVE WON!
WE WAS ROBBED!
UNFAIR!

MEANWHILE, BELOW THE STREETS OF SPRINGFIELD...
COME ON! TIME TO GET UP!
THAT'S IT. COME OUT OF HIDING. AND BECAUSE YOU STAYED HIDDEN, THERE WILL BE SECOND HELPINGS AT DINNER TONIGHT FOR ALL OF YOU.
NOW IT'S OFF TO WORK WITH YOU...
I SAY WE GO UNION. PASS IT ON!!
...AND DON'T FORGET YOUR MINING TOOLS, MY PRECIOUS LITTLE MONSTERS. BWA-HA-HA-HA!
THE END

THE CASE OF THE MISSING MOON WAFFLES

FROM THE SECRET FILES OF LISA SIMPSON

ONE MONDAY MORNING...

AAIIIEEEE!!! MY WAFFLES! MY ***DELICIOUS*** MOON WAFFLES!* THEY'RE GONE. ***GONE!*** SOMEONE ***ATE*** MY ***GLORIOUS WAFFLES!***

*TO MAKE HOMER'S PATENTED, SPACE AGE, OUT OF THIS WORLD MOON WAFFLES JUST POUR WAFFLE BATTER, CARAMEL, AND LIQUID SMOKE INTO A WAFFLE IRON. THEN WRAP THE COOKED WAFFLE AROUND A STICK OF BUTTER AND ENJOY!

DON'T LOOK AT ME! I DIDN'T TAKE HIS MOON WAFFLES. I DON'T EVEN *LIKE* THEM.
THE *CARAMEL* GETS STUCK IN MY TEETH AND THE *LIQUID SMOKE* MAKES ME BREAK OUT IN A *RASH*.

MOM, WHERE WERE YOU WHEN THE MOON WAFFLES *DISAPPEARED*?
LISA, I DON'T HAVE TIME FOR *ANOTHER* ONE OF YOUR FATHER'S *WAFFLE CRISES*. I NEED TO MAKE THESE LUNCHES, OR YOU'LL BE LATE FOR SCHOOL.

MAGGIE?...

SUCK!
SUCK!

AFTER GATHERING ALL THE *CIRCUMSTANTIAL EVIDENCE* AND WEIGHING ALL OF YOUR *ALIBIS*,
ONLY ONE PERSON COULD HAVE EATEN THE WAFFLES

IT WAS... *YOU!*

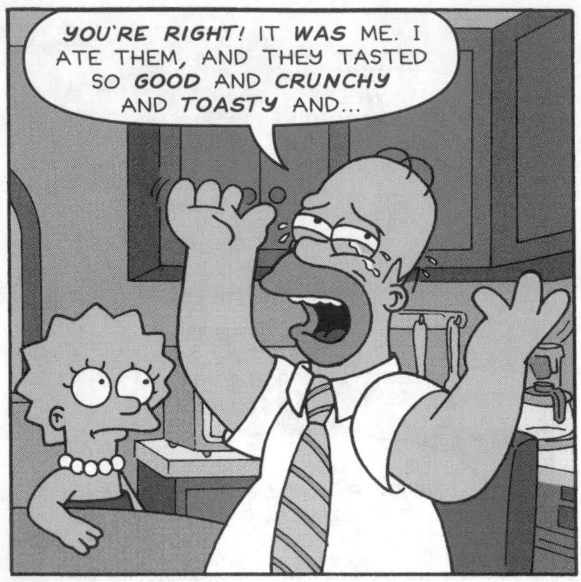

TERRY DELEGEANE STORY | MIKE WORLEY PENCILS | SCOTT MCRAE INKS | RICK REESE COLORS | KAREN BATES LETTERS | MATT GROENING MR. BUTTERWORTH

BART SIMPSON AND HIS FAMILY VISIT STAMPY THE ELEPHANT IN:

"ALL'S VELDT THAT ENDS VELDT!"

OUT OF THE *WAY*, FOLKS!

B'WANA BART THE *WILD ANIMAL-HANDLER* COMIN' THROUGH!

WHAT THE--?

OH, *MY!*

FLING!

BRUFF RUFF RUFF! BRUFF RUFF RUFF!

MEOWRRR!!!

SCOTT SHAW! STORY & PENCILS
PHYLLIS NOVIN INKS
RICK REESE COLORS
KAREN BATES LETTERS
BILL MORRISON EDITOR
MATT GROENING HEAD ZOOKEEPER

LISA, DO YOU HAVE ANY IDEA WHERE MAGGIE IS?
LISA!?!
HUH?

I ASKED YOU IF YOU KNOW WHERE MAGGIE IS!
OH, SORRY, MOM, I WAS BUSY LISTENING TO MY NEW CD BY "O-ZONE PLAYERZ"!
I THINK MAGGIE'S IN THE LIVING ROOM WATCHING TV...

♪ PORKEYMEN... ♪ GOTTA PITCH ♫ 'EM ALL... ♫
SUCK! SUCK! SUCK! SUCK!

TODAY, OUR HEROES COMPETE AGAINST A TOTALLY NEW ASSORTMENT OF WEIRD CREATURES WE HAVEN'T EVEN SOLD TO YOU...YET!
"WHAT'S NEW PORKEYMEN?"
SUCK! SUCK! SUCK! SUCK!

PIKKA-BOOGAH! SNUK-SNUK!
WOOBWOOBWOOBWOOB
WOOBWOOBWOOBWOOB

PIKKA-BOOGAH!
OH, THERE YOU ARE! COME WITH ME, MAGGIE...
SUCK! SUCK! SUCK! SUCK!
WOOBWOOBWOOBWOOB

HERE'S MAGGIE! SHE WAS JUST WATCHING ONE OF HER CARTOON SHOWS!
WHEW!
WELL, LET'S SNAP IT UP, PEOPLE! I'VE GOT A PACHYDERM WAITING FOR ME!

...LA DE DAH DE LAH...LET'S RECYCLE OUR LOVE...IN THE COMPOST OF LIFE ...LA DAH DAH DAH...
WHATEVER IT IS THAT LISA'S SINGING IS DRIVING ME NUTS!
OH, SHE'S JUST IMMERSED IN THAT NEW MUSIC CD OF HERS.
YEAH, SHE'S LISTENING TO HER FAVORITE BOY-BAND --THIS WEEK, AT LEAST!

BEFORE TOO LONG...
ALL RIGHT! STAMPY, HERE WE COME!
THAT RIDE WASN'T SO BAD, WAS IT? NOW WE CAN STRETCH OUR LEGS!
SPRINGFIELD WILD ANIMAL PARK
WELL, START STRETCHIN', MARGE!
THE EMPTY PARKING SPACES LOOK LIKE THEY'RE ABOUT THREE MILES AWAY FROM THE GATE!

THOSE ADMISSION TICKETS COST ME A SMALL FORTUNE, SO I'M EXPECTING YOU KIDS TO HAVE THE BEST TIME OF YOUR SHORT LIVES!
OH, DON'T WORRY YOUR SHINY HEAD ABOUT THAT, HOMER!

SOUVENIRS AHOY!
THE HAPPY HUNTER SOUVENIR SHOP
THE GRINNING
WHEW! I NEED TO FRESHEN UP IN THE NEAREST LADIES' ROOM! HOMER, WOULD YOU PLEASE WATCH MAGGIE?

MAN, I CAN HEAR THOSE RUBBER SNAKES CALLIN' MY NAME "BART SSSSSSSIMPSON!"
SUCK! SUCK! SUCK! SUCK!
YOU GET BACK HERE, BOY!
PLOP!

A FEW MINUTES LATER...
WHAT ARE YOU BOYS DOING IN HERE?
AW, MARGE, HE WAS TRYING TO SHAKE ME DOWN FOR A PHONY TARANTULA!
I'M JUST CHECKIN' OUT THE RUBBER SNAKES!

SOON...
STEP LIVELY, EVERYONE! THE W'GAFFA BUSH LINE* IS ABOUT TO LEAVE ON ITS AUTOMATED TOUR OF THE PARK!
ACCORDING TO THIS COLORFUL BROCHURE, THAT'S WHERE WE'LL SEE STAMPY!
LOOK, HOMER, THIS PLACE MUST BE ZONED TO SELL BEER!
DUFF BEER SOLD HERE!
THE W'GAFFA BUSH LINE
OOOH, MAYBE THEY HAVE THOSE FROSTY DUFF-SICLES!
*ACCORDING TO PRESERVE LORE, W'GAFFA IS ACTUALLY AN ACRONYM FOR "WHO GIVES A FLYIN' FIG, ANYWAY?"

WELCOME ABOARD THE W'GAFFA BUSH LINE! PLEASE KEEP YOUR HANDS INSIDE THE TRAM TO AVOID FEEDING THE ANIMALS...YOUR HANDS, THAT IS!
MMM...GAZELLE-ICIOUS!
OH, MY! ISN'T ALL THE WILDLIFE SIMPLY BREATH-TAKING, HOMER?
WELL, I THINK THEY'RE "BREATH-TAKING", MOM...ESPECIALLY SINCE NONE OF THESE WALKING MANURE-FACTORIES ARE HOUSE-BROKEN!
WHOOP! WHOOP!
RAHHHRRWW!
TOOKI-TOOKI!
BLARGHH!

HEY, LOOK...A SLOTH! NOW THERE'S AN ANIMAL I CAN REALLY RELATE TO!
YEAH, ALL IT NEEDS IS A COUCH, A TV, A BAG OF CHIPS, AND A SIX-PACK!

OH, ISN'T THAT BABY CHIMP JUST THE CUTEST THING YOU'VE EVER SEEN? SOMEHOW, IT REMINDS ME OF MAGGIE...
...MAGGIE!?! OMIGOSH, WHERE'S MAGGIE?!?

WHAT'S WRONG, MOM?
IF YOU WERE PAYING ATTENTION, YOUNG LADY, YOU'D REALIZE THAT YOUR LITTLE SISTER IS MISSING!
NOW MARGE! LET'S ALL MELLOW OUT. TAKE A LESSON FROM THE SLOTHS!
DON'T YOU SLOTH ME, HOMER! YOU'RE THE ONE WHO WAS SUPPOSED TO BE WATCHING MAGGIE!

LOOK, MOM, IT WAS MY FAULT HOMER LOST MAGGIE, SO I'LL GO FIND HER AND BRING HER BACK, SAFE 'N' SOUND!
HMMM, I DON'T KNOW IF THAT'S SUCH A GOOD IDEA...
DON'T THINK OF IT AS LOSING A SON BUT AS GAINING A DAUGHTER!
ACTUALLY, I WAS SAVING THAT THOUGHT FOR BART'S WEDDING DAY!

"WEDDING DAY?" MOM, PUH-LEASE DON'T GROSS ME OUT WHILE I'M ABOUT TO SAVE MAGGIE'S BACON!
HOP!

MEANWHILE, MAGGIE'S STILL UNDER THE INFLUENCE OF HER NEW "MASTER", PIKKANOSE...
SUCK! SUCK! SUCK! SUCK!

SHE'S THINKS SHE'S ON A MISSION FOR HIM!
PIKKA-BOOGAH! SNUK-SNUK!
SUCK! SUCK! SUCK! SUCK!

SUCK! SUCK! SUCK! SUCK!
DANGEROUS! KEEP OUT!!!

AT THE SAME TIME...
THIS DIRECTION LOOKS LIKE IT MIGHT BE A SHORT CUT BACK TO THE TRAM STATION!
WELCOME TO THE AFRICAN VELDT!
(LEGAL DISCLAIMER: NOT THE AFRICAN VELDT)

OKAAYY...NO PROBLEMS SO FARRRR...EVERYTHING'S COOOOOL...
GRRRRR

GRRRROWWWLLL
YAAAHH!!

PUFF! PANT! PUFF! PANT! PUFF! PANT!
HEY, HAVEN'T YOU GUYS EVER HEARD OF "THE CIRCLE OF LIFE"?
OF COURSE, THAT'S JUST A NICE WAY OF REFERRING TO "THE SURVIVAL OF THE FITTEST"!
D'OH!
RRROARRR!!!

MAYBE I CAN LOSE 'EM IF I CAN JUST MAKE IT ACROSS THIS CHASM!
LEAP!
GLOM!
SKIDD!
UNNGHH! GOT IT!!!

ERGHHH!
HUH?

--STAMPY!?!
EEENGHHH!
GRAB!

YOU STILL LIKE TO TREAT PEOPLE LIKE HUMAN PACIFIERS, HUH, STAMPY?
STUFF!
THEY SAY ELEPHANTS NEVER FORGET, BUT I'D SURE LIKE TO FORGET THIS! YECHHH!

MEANWHILE, MAGGIE TRIES TO CARRY OUT THE TELEVISED ORDERS OF PIKKANOSE: TO CONQUER ALL THE WILD ANIMALS SHE CAN FIND...
SUCK! SUCK! SUCK! SUCK!

MAGGIE'S FIRST OPPONENT IS A SILVERBACK BULL LOWLAND GORILLA AND HIS FAMILY...
SUCK! SUCK! SUCK! SUCK!
GRRNK?

GROOT! GROOT! GROOT!
WHAP! WHAP! WHAP! WHAP!
SUCK! SUCK! SUCK! SUCK!

SUCK! SUCK! SUCK! SUCK!
HURL!

MAGGIE'S AIM IS TRUE, STRIKING THE GORILLA ON ITS SENSITIVE NOSE...
HUH?
BWOINK!

MAGGIE IS TRIUMPHANT!
SUCK! SUCK! SUCK! SUCK!
OOH!
OOOOH!
WUG!
OOH!
PLOP!

NOT EVEN THE MIGHTY CAPE BUFFALO, THE WORLD'S MOST DANGEROUS ANIMAL, CAN WITHSTAND PIKKANOSE-MAGGIE!
SUCK! SUCK! SUCK! SUCK!
SNORRT!

NOR THE FLEET-FOOTED CHEETAH, THE WORLD'S FASTEST ANIMAL, CAN BEST PIKKANOSE-MAGGIE!
MEORRR!

AND AS FOR THE MYSTERIOUS PLATYPUS, THE WORLD'S ONLY POISONOUS WARM-BLOODED ANIMAL, IT'S NO CONTEST!
SUCK! SUCK! SUCK! SUCK!
SPA FON!

BACK ON THE TRAM...
OH, I'M A TERRIBLE MOTHER!
I'M SURE THAT SOMEWHERE THERE ARE MOTHERS EVEN WORSE THAN YOU!

AS I RECALL, MAGGIE DISAPPEARED WHILE YOU WERE SUPPOSED TO BE WATCHING HER!
YEAH, BUT THAT'S ONLY BECAUSE YOU WERE TOO BUSY "FRESHENING UP", AND LISA HERE WAS TOO BUSY LISTENING TO HER "BOZO PLAYERS" CD!
THAT'S "O-ZONE PLAYERZ," DAD.
UNH, A LITTLE HELP HERE?
AT THE RISK OF REPEATING MYSELF...
...HELP!!!

HEY, HOW ABOUT THAT--A TALKING ELEPHANT!
NO, DAD, IT'S STAMPY, AND HE'S GOT BART IN HIS MOUTH!
OMIGOSH! WE'VE GOT TO HELP HIM!
C'MON, FOLKS--LESS YAKKIN', MORE UNPACKIN'!

MAYBE I CAN BREAK OFF ONE OF THESE UHHN BRANCHES...!

AND REACH BART WITH IT FROM HERE...
WHOOPSIE!
AAAGHHH!
LISA!!!

HONEY, ARE YOU ALL RIGHT?
OOF!
YEAH, I GUESS SO...
MAYBE AFTER YOU RESCUE BART AND MAGGIE, YOU COULD HIKE BACK TO THE REFRESHMENT STAND AND GET ME A BEER?
THWUMP!

THERE GOES THE TRAM! IT'S AUTOMATED, SO THERE'S NO CHANCE OF IT STOPPING OR TURNING BACK!
AHEM! A LITTLE HELP HERE?
OH, SORRY, BART!
DUST!
DUST!

C'MON, STAMPY, SPIT OUT BART! NICE STAMPY! GOOD STAMPY!
UH, I HATE TO TELL YOU THIS, LIS', BUT STAMPY IS A SAVAGE BEAST!

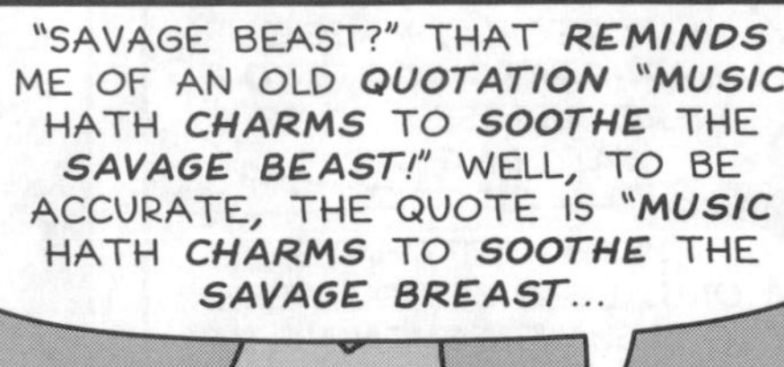

"SAVAGE BEAST?" THAT REMINDS ME OF AN OLD QUOTATION "MUSIC HATH CHARMS TO SOOTHE THE SAVAGE BEAST!" WELL, TO BE ACCURATE, THE QUOTE IS "MUSIC HATH CHARMS TO SOOTHE THE SAVAGE BREAST...

YOUR EARS ARE A LOT BIGGER THAN THESE HEADPHONES WERE DESIGNED FOR, STAMPY!
CLIP!
WHATCHA DOIN', LISA? YOU GONNA PUNISH STAMPY BY MAKING HIM LISTEN TO "THE O-ZONE PLAYERZ"?

♪ ...LA DE DAH DE ♪ LAH...LET'S RECYCLE OUR LOVE...IN THE COMPOST OF LIFE...LA ♪ DAH DAH DAH... ♪

BART! YOU'RE ALL RIGHT!
WELL, I'VE ALWAYS THOUGHT SO!
EWWW!!! YOU'RE ALL SLIMY WITH ELEPHANT SPIT!
YEAH! COOL, HUH?
SPTOOEY!

LOOK OUT, LIS'! I'M GONNA GET ELEPHANT SLOBBER ON YOU!
NEVER MIND THAT, BART! WE'VE GOTTA FIND MAGGIE AND FAST!

MEANWHILE, A PACK OF LAUGHING HYENAS ARE COMPLETELY IMMUNE TO MAGGIE'S "PORKEYMEN" TECHNIQUES...
SUCK! SUCK! SUCK! SUCK!
YEEHEE HEEHEE!!!
HYUK-HYUK-HYUK!

BUT THEY DO THINK SHE'S JUST ABOUT THE TASTIEST-LOOKING LITTLE MORSEL THEY'VE EVER SEEN!
YEEHEEHEE SLURP!-- YEEHEEHEE!!!

YEEHEEHEEHEE!!!
SUCK! SUCK! SUCK! SUCK!

SUCK! SUCK! SUCK! SUCK!
SLURP!

SUCK! SUCK! SUCK! SUCK!
YANK!
SNAP!

WHOA, MAMA! STAMP 'EM, STAMPY!
HREENK!!!
SUCK!! SUCK!! SUCK!! SUCK!!
STOMP!
BASH!
YI!
YI!
YI!
YI!
YI!
YI!

BACK AT THE TRAM STATION...
I'M NOT BUDGING UNTIL I'M REUNITED WITH OUR POOR, LOST CHILDREN!
AW, C'MON, MARGE! THEY'LL TURN UP EVENTUALLY!

HIIII-YO, STAMPY!
HI, MOM AND DAD! STAMPY HELPED US FIND MAGGIE!
SUCK!! SUCK!! SUCK!! SUCK!!

OH, MAGGIE, MY SWEET, WONDERFUL LITTLE BABY! I'M SO GLAD YOU'RE SAFE!
SUCK!! SUCK!! SUCK!! SUCK!!

UH, MARGE, I THINK SOME "TOUGH LOVE" PARENTING IS IN ORDER!
MAGGIE, YOU WERE A VERY BAD GIRL TO RUN OFF LIKE THAT! BAD GIRL, MAGGIE!
MAGGIE USES HER PORKEYMEN TECHNIQUE ONE LAST TIME...ON STAMPY!

DON'T LOOK SO DOWN IN THE MOUTH, HOMER! DON'T YOU REALIZE HOW FEW PEOPLE EVER GET TO SEE AN ELEPHANT'S UVULA?
HEY!
ERGHHH!
STUFF!
THE END

APPROVED BY THE COMICS CODE AUTHORITY
SIMPSONS COMICS PRESENTS
BART SIMPSON
LITTLE RASCAL
#8
US $2.50
CAN $3.50
MATT GROENING
J.HO
REESE
©2002 BONGO ENTERTAINMENT, INC. THE SIMPSONS ©&TM TCFFC. ALL RIGHTS RESERVED.

BART SIMPSON... THE TIME HAS *FINALLY* COME...

...TO THROW THE *BOOK* AT YOU.

THE DICKENS YOU SAY

I'M NOT GONNA SWEAT IT, MILHOUSE.
WHAT ARE YOU TALKING ABOUT? IT'S DUE TOMORROW.
IT'S A NEW WORLD WE LIVE IN, MY FRIEND.

THE AGE OF MULTI-MEDIA.

SOON...
THE ANDROID'S DUNGEON & BASEBALL CARD SHOP
HOW MUCH IS THAT CLASSICS ADUMBRATED COPY OF "GREAT EXPECTATIONS", MY MAN?
THIS COPY?
"TAKE ME TO YOUR COMIC BOOK & BASEBALL CARDS"
YES WE'RE OPEN

THIS COPY IS SIGNED BY NONE OTHER THAN HAL KILBY, THE CREATOR OF BUTTERFLY GIRL AND THE EMERALD SQUAB.
HAL KILBY DREW THIS?
TOFUMAN
GREAT EXPECTATION
KID SELTZER
RHINO GIRL

SADLY NO. IT ILLUSTRATES THE FOLLY OF SENDING YOUR MOTHER TO A COMIC CONVENTION TO ACQUIRE AUTOGRAPHS. IT WAS THE LEGENDARY SHELBYVILLE COMIC-FEST. I CAME DOWN WITH A CHILD-HOOD ILLNESS AND COULD...
COMICS
GREAT EXPECTATIONS

LONG STORY SHORT. YOU WANT TO SOAK ME FOR IT.
A KING'S RANSOM WOULD BE A MERE DOWN PAYMENT.
SIGH.

SO MUCH FOR THAT PLAN, BART.
I'M DOWN BUT NOT OUT, MILHOUSE.
I'VE BARELY BEGUN TO SCRATCH THE SURFACE OF THE MEDIA RESOURCES AT MY DISPOSAL.

I NOW TURN TO THE MAN WHO CAN MAKE ANY DREAM COME TRUE.

WELL, KIDS, LET'S GIVE A GREAT BIG ROUND OF KRUSTY APPLAUSE TO JACK SAFARI AND HIS CIRCUS OF CARRION EATERS!
I'M NOT DEAD!
I TELL YOU I'M NOT, YOU FOUL BEAST!

SOMETHING SPECIAL NEXT, KIDLETS. IT'S NOT OFTEN WE TAKE REQUESTS ON THIS SHOW. BUT ONE LITTLE TYKE CALLED TO TELL ME THAT HE'S ONLY GOT ONE WEEK TO LIVE.

AND THE ONE THING THAT WOULD SEND HIM INTO THE AFTERLIFE WITH A SMILE ON HIS FACE WOULD BE HIS FAVORITE CARTOON.
WHAT'S A CLOWN TO DO?

THIS ONE'S FOR YOU, BART SIMPSON.
THIS ISN'T GOING TO WORK, BART.
WATCH AND LEARN, LIS. WATCH AND LEARN.

ITCHY & SCRATCHY
Great Expectorations

CARNIVAL TODAY!

WIN
$$$

WIN
$100

P-TOO!

WIN

WIN
$1,000,000,000

GAAAAASP!

P-TOO!

THUD!

HEE!
HEE!
HEE!

LET ME GUESS...
...THAT WAS NOT AN ACCURATE ADAPTATION OF THE DICKENS CLASSIC.
HA! HA! HA! HA!

YOU ONLY HAVE A FEW MORE HOURS UNTIL BEDTIME, AND YOU PINNED YOUR HOPES ON A CARTOON!
I'LL ADMIT DISAPPOINTMENT BUT NEVER DEFEAT!

DAD, YOU HAVE TO TAKE ME TO THE VIDEO DEN!
NOT NOW, BOY! I'M RIGHT IN THE MIDDLE OF SOME-THING.

ONE MORE PEA ADDED TO THIS STACK AND I'LL HAVE BROKEN MY PERSONAL RECORD.
BUT IT'S FOR SCHOOL, HOMER.

YOU HEARD HIM, HOMER. IT'S FOR SCHOOL.
SURE. THAT EXCUSE.
HIS EDUCATION COMES BEFORE MY DREAMS.

NO!

VIDEO DEN
RENT ONE STEVEN SEAGAL AND GET THREE SYLVESTER STALLONES FREE.
McBAIN XII
JAWS

YOU CAN'T RENT THIS.
YOU MEAN IT'S *OUT*?
NO. IT'S RATED "R".

WHO *KNEW* THERE WERE SO MANY POLICE DOG MOVIES? WHAT A COUNTRY.
DAD, YOU GOTTA *HELP* ME! THE MOVIE I NEED FOR *SCHOOL* IS RATED "R"!
WOLF

WE'VE HAD THIS DISCUSSION *BEFORE*, YOUNG MAN.
WE'RE NOT HAVING THAT *FILTH* IN OUR HOUSE.
AW, MAN...

SO, THE MOVIE THE KID WANTS IS FOR *ADULTS*, EH? ANY *NUDITY*?
YEAH. GWYNETH PALTROW.

AW, MAN...
VHS

HO, HO. I HEARD YOUR LATEST DODGE WENT DOWN IN FLAMES.
STUPID RATINGS SYSTEM.
HOW'S A KID SUPPOSED TO LEARN ANYTHING?

OH, I DON'T KNOW... YOU COULD TRY ACTUALLY READING THE BOOK.

LIKE YOU'VE ACTUALLY READ "GREAT EXAGGERATIONS".
AS A MATTER OF FACT, I HAVE.
I'LL BET YOU HAVEN'T.

I HAVE!
I READ IT!
GET REAL.
IN YOUR DREAMS.
I'LL PROVE IT TO YOU!

HEH, HEH. SPEAK INTO THE HIDDEN MIKE, LITTLE SISTER.

GREAT EXPECTATIONS BY CHARLES DICKENS.
PIP IS AN ORPHAN BOY WHO RECEIVES A MYSTERIOUS ENDOWMENT...
RAP ON, BRAINIAC.

TWO HOURS GO BY...
...AND SO WITH THE MYSTERY SOLVED, PIP FACES HIS FUTURE WITH HIS PAST EXPLAINED, AND A LOVE TO SHARE HIS LIFE WITH. THE END.
WHUH?
UH...I GUESS YOU'RE ***RIGHT***, LIS. YOU ***DID*** READ IT.

NOT THAT IT HELPS ***YOU*** ANY, BART. GOOD LUCK WRITING THAT BOOK REPORT BEFORE ***BEDTIME***.
LUCK HAS ***NOTHING*** TO DO WITH IT.
VAN

MAN. THIS IS ***MORE*** BORING THE SECOND TIME.
BLAH BLAH BLAH BLAH BLAH BLAH...

WELL, THIS REPORT ISN'T UP TO ***LISA'S*** STANDARDS, BUT IT'S A SLAM DUNK "A" FOR YOURS TRULY.

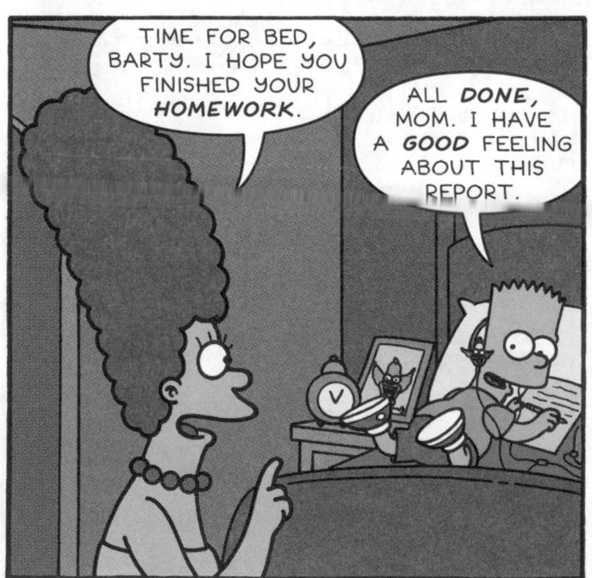
TIME FOR BED, BARTY. I HOPE YOU FINISHED YOUR ***HOMEWORK***.
ALL ***DONE***, MOM. I HAVE A ***GOOD*** FEELING ABOUT THIS REPORT.

SO DO I, BROTHER.
SO DO ***I***.

THE NEXT MORNING...
SO, DID YOU GET THE **REPORT** FINISHED?
IN THE **BAG,** MILHOUSE, MY MAN.
HOW'D YOU **DO** IT? DID YOU GO ON THE **INTERNET**?

NOTHING SO **PRIMITIVE**.
I USED **SUBTERFUGE**.
IS THAT LIKE **RITALIN**?

YOU'RE **NEXT** ON THE LIST, BART.
I HAVE MY REPORT RIGHT **HERE,** TEACH.

"GREAT EXPECTATIONS" BY CHARLES DICKENS.
THIS IS THE STORY OF A GUY NAMED PIP WHO WAS AN ORPHAN. AND WHEN HE GETS TO VOTING AGE HE GETS SENT TO LONDON...

...THAT'S WHERE HE MEETS **JAMES BOND**. EVEN THOUGH HE HAS A **STUPID** NAME, THEY LET HIM BECOME A **SPY** AND HIS FIRST MISSION IS TO **AUSTRALIA** WHERE SOME MYSTERIOUS GUY IS PLANTING BOMBS IN KANGAROO'S POUCHES.

FIVE MINUTES LATER...
...AND SO PIP THROWS MR. BUMBLECHOOK OFF THE EIFFEL TOWER AND THEN MARRIES MOLLY HAVERSHAM ON MTV.

CHUCK DIXON SCRIPT · DAN DECARLO LAYOUTS · MIKE KAZALEH PENCILS · MIKE ROTE INKS · ART VILLANUEVA COLORS · KAREN BATES LETTERS · MATT GROENING SPEED READER

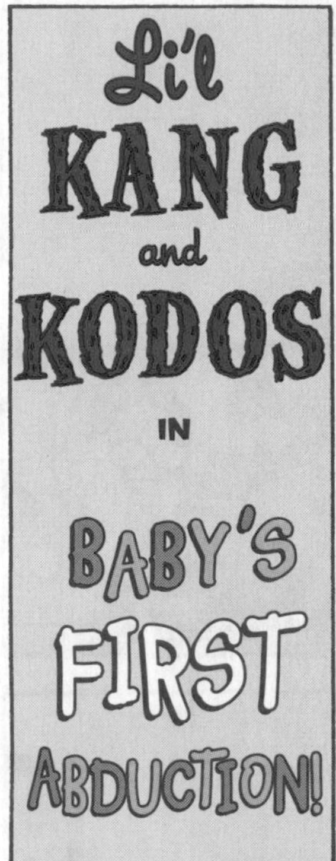

GAIL SIMONE SCRIPT · DAN DECARLO LAYOUTS · MIKE ROTE PENCILS · ANDREW PEPOY INKS · ART VILLANUEVA COLORS · KAREN BATES LETTERS · BILL MORRISON EDITS · MATT GROENING TANK CLEANER

EIGHT YEARS LATER, AS THE PRECOCIOUS TYKES GROW UP...
HAPPY 8TH LUNAR CYCLE, KANG AND KODOS!
IT IS JUST WHAT I HAVE MOST DESIRED! THANK YOU, PARENTAL UNITS!
BUT I WANTED A SPACE PONY!
MY FIRST SAUCER

OH, PLEASE, MAY WE USE THE SAUCER TO ABDUCT SOMEONE, PLEASE, PLEASE, PLEASE?
WELL...I SUPPOSE IT IS ALL RIGHT.
BUT STAY WITHIN ONE MILLION LIGHT YEARS!

WOOOOOOSHHH!*
WHEEEEEEE!
AHA! HERE IS A PLANET RIPE FOR INVASION! NOW WE MUST FIND A SUITABLE VICTIM FOR EXTRACTING INFORMATION!
*YEAH, WE KNOW THERE'S NO SOUND IN SPACE. BUT THEY'RE GOING REALLY FAST!--STAR RANGER BILL

DO YOU THINK THAT THIS CONTAINMENT POD MAKES ME LOOK FAT?
THIS EARTHLING SEEMS TO BE SURROUNDED BY WEALTH. HE MUST BE THE LEADER! LET US ABDUCT HIM!
Monty
M

THIS STORY IS DEDICATED TO THE MOST HEROIC ***STUFFED ANIMAL*** OF ALL! THANKS FROM ALL OF US HERE AT BONGO TO BRAVE, BRAVE ***BOBO!***

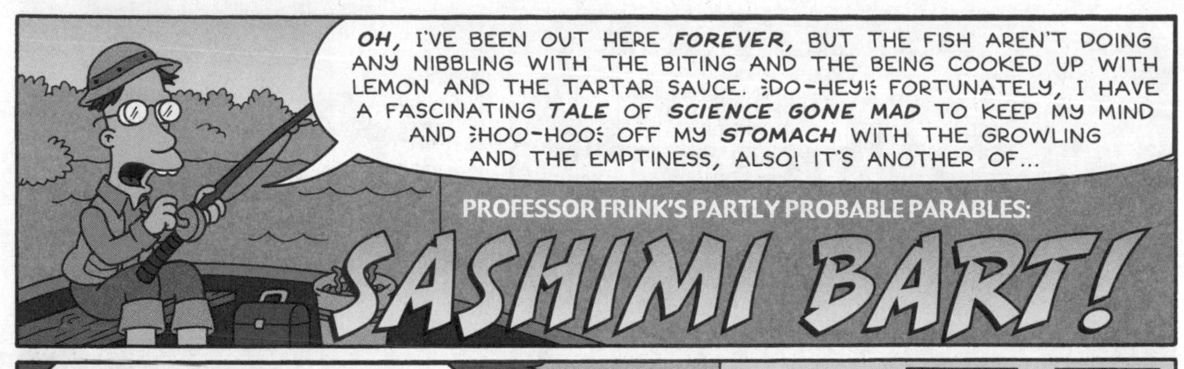

BART, I JUST WOULD LIKE TO ***THANK*** YOU FOR HELPING WITH THE WASHING AND SUDSING OF MY NEW ***POGO-MOBILE***.

AS YOU KNOW, IT'S THE ONLY VEHICLE TO HARNESS THE AWESOME POWER OF ***POGO***.

I CALL IT THE ***UP-CHUCK TRUCK***.

YES, AND ***I*** WISH YOU'D ***STOP***. NG-HEY!

SPRINGFIE
INSTITUTE
SCIENCE
DRIVE-THRU OPEN
TIL MIDNIGHT!

GAIL SIMONE	***DAN DECARLO***	***JASON HO***	***ART VILLANUEVA***	***KAREN BATES***	***MATT GROENING***
STORY	LAYOUTS	PENCILS/INKS	COLORS	LETTERS	CATCH OF THE DAY

GOTTA GET SOME COVER... I'LL HIDE IN THE LAB!
CORE PROGRAMMING DEMANDS CONTINUED IMMERSION OF HUMAN CHILD!
RETURN FOR ADDITIONAL SPLASHING, HUMAN!

HEH...NEVER GET IN A WATER FIGHT WITH A SCIENTIST.
HE'LL BE SAFE IN THE LAB, OF COURSE. THERE'S ABSOLUTELY NO DANGER, AS LONG AS HE DOESN'T...

...PUSH THE BUTTON ON MY AMPHIBIAN TRANS-MUTATION MACHINE!
?
OH, FOR THE LOVE OF LIMPET!

BART! YOUR MOTHER IS STILL MAD AT ME FOR THAT TIME I ACCIDENTALLY TURNED YOU INTO A PARAMECIUM. YOU'RE DELIBERATELY TRYING TO GET ME IN TROUBLE WITH THE YELLING AND THE LAWSUITS AND THE CALLING OF NAMES!
I'M SORRY, PROFESSOR!

SPLASH THE HUMAN!
NOT NOW, YOU IDIOT!

...AND SO WHAT YOU'RE TELLING ME IS THAT MY SON IS NOW A **FISH**?
ER.....YES. SORRY.
SAY, IS YOUR WIFE GOING TO BE ALL RIGHT WHAT WITH THE **PASSING OUT** AND **FALLING** TO THE **FLOOR**?
EH. I'LL GET HER A PILLOW LATER.

MAGGIE! DON'T FEED HIM TOO MUCH, OR HE'LL DIE!

WELL, I'M CERTAIN YOU HAVE A LOT OF BREADING AND PAN-FRYING...UH, ER, I MEAN **CATCHING UP** TO DO, SO I'LL JUST LEAVE BEFORE YOUR WIFE **WAKES UP** AND STARTS **HITTING** ON ACCOUNT OF I BRUISE EASILY AND THE **AMBULANCE** CHARGING AN ARM AND A LEG ⁞HOO!⁞
ER...GOODBYE, YES.

SOON...
OH, WHAT A **HORRIBLE DREAM**.

THAT'S NOT LIKE ME, TO TAKE A SIESTA IN THE MIDDLE OF THE DAY, **PARTICULARLY** ON THE LIVING ROOM FLOOR. I'D BETTER GET TO CLEANING THE BATHROOM, AS SCHEDULED!
LESS TALK, MORE SPOCK!

HI, MOM! DAD SAYS THIS IS MY NEW BEDROOM!
OH MY **WORD!**

THE NEXT MORNING...
NO...WE ARE NOT SELLING OUR SON TO THE CIRCUS, AND THAT'S FINAL.
GOOD THINKING, MARGE! WHY LET THOSE SLEAZY RINGMASTERS MAKE ALL THE MONEY?
WE'LL JUST CHARGE THE RUBES FIVE BUCKS A POP TO LOOK AT HIM IN THE BATHROOM! LISA CAN SELL CORN DOGS! OF COURSE, SHE'LL HAVE TO QUIT SCHOOL...

I'M NOT QUITTING SCHOOL TO SELL CORN DOGS, DAD! BESIDES, WE NEED THAT BATHTUB, SOME OF US MORE THAN OTHERS!
WELL, I CERTAINLY CAN'T QUIT SCHOOL. I DON'T EVEN GO TO SCHOOL!

AWWW, CAN'T I JUST BE A CRIME-FIGHTING FREAK?
THERE'LL BE NO CRIME-FIGHTING OR FREAKISM IN THIS HOUSE, YOUNG MAN!

OH, HOW ADORABLE! MAGGIE KISSED BART'S BOWL! GOOD BABY!
BART, I'M SORRY, BUT I'M AFRAID YOU'RE GOING TO HAVE TO GO TO SCHOOL JUST LIKE ANY OTHER KID.
SMECK!

BUT HOW ABOUT I MAKE YOU A NICE PLATE OF PANCAKES, OKAY? THEY'RE YOUR FAVORITE!
UGH...

:SIGH: ALL RIGHT, YOU CAN HAVE WORMS ON YOUR PANCAKES.
YUM!

LATER...
BART! I ASKED YOU A QUESTION. ARE YOU EVEN LISTENING?
NICE FISH BOWL, FISH BOWL HEAD. HA, HA!
HAWLEY SMOOT and YOU

WELL, IT'S KINDA HARD CONCENTRATING WITH THIS SEA CAPTAIN STARING AT ME ALL THE TIME!
HAWLEY SMOOT and YOU

FLOUNDER FACE! FLOUNDER FACE!
I'M SORRY, BART. BUT MY MOM SAYS I SHOULDN'T BE FRIENDS WITH A FISH! I COULD GET FIN ROT!

MAN, THIS STINKS LIKE MACKEREL. WHY COULDN'T I HAVE GOTTEN A USEFUL MUTATION, LIKE A SHRUNKEN HEAD OR EARS THAT THROW LIGHTNING BOLTS?
SPROING!
SPROING!
ARF!
ARF!

BART! THIS IS A MATTER OF LIFE OR DEATH! THERE'S A CAPSIZED SHIP AND THE FLOODING IS UP TO HERE WITH WATER AND THE ICY COLD. BRRRRRRR!
ONLY YOU
THE CREW!
WELL, THEN, WHAT ARE WE WAITING FOR?
WHOA, DUDE!
AWESOME!

THE ONLY WAY IN IS THROUGH THE PORTHOLES, BART, AND THE RESCUE DIVERS ARE ALL TOO BIG! HOY! TAKE THESE OXYGEN MASKS AND FIND A WAY FOR THE CREW TO GET OUT!
UH...CAN'T WE THINK THIS THROUGH A LITTLE?

ER, NO!
POOT!
WAAUUGHH!
SPLOOOOSH!

LOUSY FRINK. KICKING ME OUT OF THE POGO-MOBILE!
GOOD THING I CAN BREATHE UNDERWATER. NOW IF ONLY I CAN FIGURE A WAY TO GET THESE GUYS OUT.

THE MINUTES ARE TICKING BY, AS OUR PLUCKY LITTLE FISH-BOY IS CAUGHT IN A RACE AGAINST TIME TRYING TO RESCUE THE BRAVE CREW OF THE S.S. MINI-TITANIC. BOY, WHAT IDIOT THOUGHT UP THAT NAME?
OH, MY SPECIAL LITTLE FISH-GUY!

THERE THEY ARE! HE'S DONE IT! HE'S DONE IT!
HOORAY! THREE CHEERS FOR BART!
GASP!
WHOA! WHO KNEW THAT A BOAT WOULD HAVE A TRAP DOOR?

BART! YOU DID IT! YOU SAVED THOSE MEN!
THAT'S NOT ALL, MOM! LOOK AT THIS OLD CHEST I FOUND WHILE I WAS DOWN THERE!

BACK AT HOME...
GREAT NEWS, SIMPSON FAMILY! I'VE DEVELOPED AN ANTIDOTE THAT'LL CHANGE BART BACK TO HIS OLD RASCALLY SELF. GLAVIN!
I'M SURE GLAD THAT PIRATE GOLD THAT BART FOUND HASN'T CHANGED US AT ALL...
♫ WE'RE NOT ♫ LISTENING!!!

THE END

BART & MILHOUSE'S ALMOST EXCELLENT ADVENTURE

OH, MAN! ANOTHER CRUDDY CLASS TRIP TO A BORING MUSEUM! WHY CAN'T WE EVER GO ANYPLACE COOL?

YEAH, LIKE TO A BROADWAY MUSICAL!

EARL KRESS SCRIPT · DAN DECARLO LAYOUTS · JASON HO PENCILS/INKS · ART VILLANUEVA COLORS · KAREN BATES LETTERS · MATT GROENING HILLBILLY AT HEART

BRUCKER'S GENERAL STORE
HEY, BART, WHAT'S A "GENERAL STORE"?

I'LL BET THEY SELL **MILITARY STUFF** TO **GENERALS!** MAYBE WE COULD BUY SOME **LEFTOVER NUKES** THERE!
WOW! THINK WHAT **THOSE** WOULD DO TO THE TOILETS AT SCHOOL!

AWW, HECK! IT'S JUST A DUMB OLD STORE LIKE THE KWIK-E-MART!
WELL, THEN LET US HAVE **TWO SQUISHEES,** PLEASE, MY MAN!
SQUISHEES? THE ONLY THING I GOT THAT'S SQUISHY IS A **RAG SOAKED IN TURPENTINE!**

NO, NO, A SQUISHEE IS LIKE **CRUSHED UP ICE** WITH **FLAVORED GOO** SWIRLED IN!
OHHH, YOU OUGHTA TRY OUR LOCAL TREAT, **CHIP-PED ICE ON TOAST!** HERE YA GO!

THIS IS **HARD WORK**...AND **COLD,** TOO!
QUIT GRIPING AND AIM FOR THE TOAST!
TINK!
TINK!

CHIPPED ICE ON TOAST! BOY, ONLY A **HALF-HOUR** OUT OF SPRINGFIELD AND EVERYTHING IS **SO DIFFERENT** HERE!
HEY, MILHOUSE, LET'S **DITCH** THIS FIELD TRIP!

NO, BART! OH, MAN! OH, MAN! OH, MAN!
KEEP IT TOGETHER, MILHOUSE! IT'S NOT LIKE THIS IS THE FIRST TIME WE'VE DITCHED A DOPEY SCHOOL THING!

IT'S NOT THAT! NOW I SEE WHY EVERYBODY LOOKS THAT WAY IN THERE! I LOST A TOOTH ON THAT STUPID CHIPPED ICE! OW! OW! OW!
HA, HA, HA! COOL!
CLUNK!

21...22...23...CLOSE ENOUGH! LET'S HIT THE ROAD, OTTO!
FAR OUT!
GRIND!

WHAT DO WE DO NOW? WE'RE OUT IN THE MIDDLE OF NOWHERE!
I SPY A COUPLE OF LOCAL YOKELS! LET'S HECKLE THEM FOR A WHILE!

HEY, HAYSEEDS! WHA'CHA UP TO? DOING HARD TIME FOR MISSING THE MORNING HOG SLOPPING?
ARE YOU KIDDIN', KID? THAT'S MY SECOND FAVORITE PART OF THE DAY!
WINK!

I'M MAX AND THIS HERE'S COUSIN SAM, AND OUR *FAVORITEST* GAME TO PLAY IS *THIS* HERE ONE! WE SEE WHO CAN *COVER THE FENCE FIRST,* WITHOUT MISSING A SPOT!
WANNA TRY? T'AIN'T AS EASY AS IT LOOKS, BUT IT SHORE IS *FUNNERIFFIC!*

TOM...HUCK... *THIS* SCAM WENT OUT WITH *VANILLA ICE! I'LL* SHOW YOU HOW TO HAVE *FUN* PAINTING THE FENCE!

SOON...
YOU WAS *RIGHT,* BART! THIS SHORE *IS* FUN!
YEAH! NEXT, CAN WE TRY SOME OF THAT THERE *VANILLY ICE*?
SPLOOP!
SLORSH!
SPLAT!
SQUINCH!

ALWAYS SIGN YOUR WORK, BOYS!
EL Barto

THANKS FOR HELPIN' US FINISH OUR CHORES.
YOU WANNA SAIL OUR BOAT IN THE CRICK WITH US?
THAT'S *KID STUFF!* I'LL SHOW YOU WHAT THE *BIG BOYS* PLAY WITH!

NAILING A SKATE TO A BOARD? WHA'JA SAY THEY CALLS THAT AGIN?
WHEN BART DOES IT, THEY CALL IT "ART"!

EAT MY DUST, RUBES!

LOOKY THERE!
GO, BART!
WAL, I'LL BE HORNSWOG-GLED!
WHIZZZ!
FLOOM!
CHUNK!

GIVE 'ER A GO, SAM THE SHAM!
GULP OKAY, I RECKON!
WHOOZ!
FLORP!

HE WRECKONED, ALL RIGHT!
IS I DAID?
YOU FLEWED, COUSIN SAM!

LET'S GO INTO THE HOUSE. I'LL SHOW YOU A GAME THAT'S NOT QUITE SO DANGEROUS!

SOON, AT A NEARBY TAVERN...
JERKW
SALOO
HELLO, JERKWATER SALOON...CORNY SPEAKING.

CAN YOU SEE IF I.M. DAMP IS THERE?
JUST A SECOND, I'LL CHECK.

I.M. DAMP. I.M. DAMP! DOES ANYONE SEE I.M. DAMP?
NOT WITH YOUR APRON ON, CORNY!

WHY YOU LITTLE DELINQUENT! IF I EVER GET MY HANDS ON YOU, I'LL MAKE YOU PAINT THE BAR!

HOPPIN' HORN TOADS, BART! YOU SHORE KNOWS HOW TO HAVE FUN!
THERE ARE THE BOYS THAT DEFACED CITY PROPERTY!
MAYOR

OKAY, SAM AND MAX, TIME TO PAY FOR YOUR SHENANIGANS!
BUT HOW'D YOU KNOWED IT WAS US?
MAYOR MAYNOT!

JUST CALL IT A HUNCH!
El Sammo
EL Barto
La Maxie

NOW YOU'RE GOING TO PAINT THE FENCE AGAIN... AND KEEP PAINTING IT UNTIL I SAY YOU'RE DONE!
YES, SIR.

HA, HA, HA! THEY SURE HAVE A THING FOR PAINT IN THIS TOWN!
UH, BART...

UH-OH.

YOU KNOW, BART, MAYBE THIS COULD BE FUN!
AW, PIPE DOWN AND PAINT!
EL BARTO
THE END

Bart Simpson

Trash Thrasher

Matt Groening